BASIC

ENGLISH GRAMMAR

Third Edition

WORKBOOK
Volume B

Betty Schrampfer Azar
Stacy A. Hagen

Basic English Grammar, Third Edition
Workbook, Volume B

Pearson Education, 10 Bank Street, White Plains, NY 10606

Staff credits: The people who made up the **Basic English Grammar
Workbook, Volume B, Third Edition** team, representing editorial, production,
design, and manufacturing, are Janice L. Baillie, Nancy Flaggman, Margo Grant,
Melissa Leyva, Robert Ruvo, and Pat Wosczyk.

Azar Associates
Shelley Hartle, Editor
Susan Van Etten, Manager

Text design and composition: Carlisle Publishing Services
Text font: 11/13.5 Plantin
Illustrations: Don Martinetti

LONGMAN ON THE WEB

Longman.com offers online resources for
teachers and students. Access our Companion
Websites, our online catalog, and our local
offices around the world.

Visit us at **longman.com.**

ISBN: 0-13-184936-0

Printed in the United States of America
1 2 3 4 5 6 7 8 9 10-BAH-11 10 09 08 07 06

Contents

Chapter 10   EXPRESSING FUTURE TIME, PART 1

Chapter 11   EXPRESSING FUTURE TIME, PART 2

PRACTICES

Chapter 12 MODALS, PART 1: EXPRESSING ABILITY

Chapter 13 MODALS, PART 2: ADVICE, NECESSITY, REQUESTS, SUGGESTIONS

PRACTICES

Chapter 14   NOUNS AND MODIFIERS

PRACTICES

Chapter 15   POSSESSIVES

Chapter 16   MAKING COMPARISONS

Preface

The *Basic English Grammar Workbook* is a place for students to explore and practice English grammar on their own. All of the exercises have been designed for independent study; they range from the basic to the more challenging to give students a chance to better understand and use English meaningfully and correctly. This book is also a resource for teachers who need exercise material for additional classwork, homework, testing, or individualized instruction.

The *Workbook* is keyed to the explanatory grammar charts found in *Basic English Grammar, Third Edition,* a classroom teaching text for students of English as a second or foreign language.

The answers to the practices can be found in the *Answer Key* in the back of the *Workbook.* Its pages are perforated so they can be detached to make a separate booklet. However, if teachers want to use the *Workbook* as a classroom teaching text, the *Answer Key* can be removed at the beginning of the term.

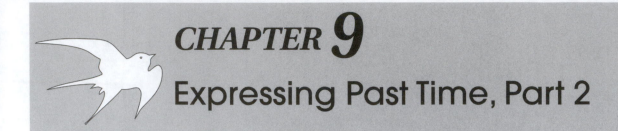

CHAPTER 9
Expressing Past Time, Part 2

◇ PRACTICE 1. WHERE, WHEN, WHAT TIME, WHY. (Chart 9-1)
Directions: Make past tense questions and answers. Use **Where . . . go?, When|What time
. . . leave?, Why . . . go there?** and the given information.

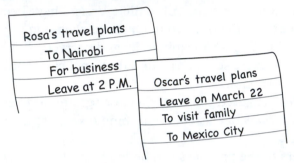

Rosa's travel plans
To Nairobi
For business
Leave at 2 P.M.

Oscar's travel plans
Leave on March 22
To visit family
To Mexico City

ROSA'S PLANS

1. A: _____ *Where did Rosa go?* _____

   B: _____ *She went to Nairobi.* _____

2. A: _____

   B: _____

3. A: _____

   B: _____

OSCAR'S PLANS

4. A: _____

   B: _____

5. A: _____

   B: _____

6. A: _____

   B: _____

◇ **PRACTICE 2. WHERE, WHEN, WHAT TIME, WHY. (Chart 9-1)**
   Directions: Write the letter of the correct response next to the question.

COLUMN A	COLUMN B
1. __B__ Who did you invite to your party?	A. A new TV.
2. _____ What time did your plane arrive?	✓B. My best friends.
3. _____ Why did you eat two breakfasts?	C. In 2003.
4. _____ When did you travel to Peru?	D. In Toronto.
5. _____ Where did you live during high school?	E. Because I was very hungry.
6. _____ What did you buy?	F. A few minutes ago.

◇ **PRACTICE 3. WHERE, WHEN, WHAT TIME, WHY. (Chart 9-1)**
   Directions: Make questions for the given answers.

   1. A: _____ *Where did you study last night?* _____
      B: At the library. (I studied at the library last night.)

   2. A: _____
      B: At 10:00. (I left the library at 10:00.)

   3. A: _____
      B: Because it closed at 10:00. (I left because the library closed at 10:00.)

   4. A: _____
      B: To the park. (My friends and I went to the park yesterday afternoon.)

   5. A: _____
      B: At Emerhoff's Shoe Store. (I got my sandals at Emerhoff's Shoe Store.)

   6. A: _____
      B: Because he was sick. (Bobby was in bed because he was sick.)

   7. A: _____
      B: Because he didn't get enough sleep. (Bobby was sick because he didn't get enough sleep.)

   8. A: _____
      B: Two days ago. (Sandra got back from Brazil two days ago.)

◇ **PRACTICE 4. WHY DIDN'T. (Chart 9-1)**
   Directions: Make questions. Begin with ***Why didn't***.

   1. A: I waited for your phone call last night. _____ *Why didn't you call?* _____
      B: Because I lost your phone number.

   2. A: It was a good movie. _____
      B: Because I needed to stay home and study.

3. A: The teacher wanted to help you. _____

   B: Because I was afraid to ask for help.

4. A: You didn't do your homework. _____

   B: Because I wanted to watch a movie.

5. A: There's no food for dinner. _____

   B: Because I didn't have time to go shopping.

6. A: Your bedroom is very messy. _____

   B: Because I was too tired.

◇ **PRACTICE 5. WHAT + verb review. (Chart 9-2)**

   Directions: Make questions. Pay attention to verb tenses.

   1. A: _____*What did you buy?*_____

      B: A digital camera. (We bought a digital camera.)

   2. A: _____*Did you buy a digital camera?*_____

      B: Yes, we did. (We bought a digital camera.)

   3. A: _____

      B: Math. (I studied math.)

   4. A: _____

      B: Yes, I did. (I studied math.)

   5. A: _____

      B: A map. (They're looking at a map.)

   6. A: _____

      B: Yes, they are. (They're looking at a map.)

   7. A: _____

      B: English grammar. (I dreamed about English grammar last night.)

   8. A: _____

      B: Yes, she is. (She's interested in science.)

   9. A: _____

      B: Science. (She's interested in science.)

  10. A: _____

      B: His country. (David talked about his country.)

  11. A: _____

      B: Yes, he did. (David talked about his country.)

  12. A: _____

      B: Nothing in particular. (I'm thinking about nothing in particular.)

13. A: _____

   B: Nothing special. (*Nothing in particular* means "nothing special.")

14. A: _____

   B: Spiders. (I am afraid of spiders.)

◇ **PRACTICE 6. Understanding questions with WHO. (Chart 9-3)**
   Directions: Write questions and short answers for the given sentences.

1. Julie called the police.

   a. Who called _____*the police?*_____ Julie.

   b. Who did _____*Julie call?*_____ The police.

2. The children visited Sara.

   a. Who visited _____ The children.

   b. Who did _____ Sara.

3. Janet helped the new manager.

   a. Who did _____ The new manager.

   b. Who helped _____ _____

4. Professor Jones taught the advanced students.

   a. Who taught _____ Professor Jones.

   b. Who did _____ _____

5. The police caught the thief.

   a. Who did _____ _____

   b. Who caught _____ _____

6. Tommy dreamed about a monster.

   a. Who dreamed about _____ _____

   b. Who did _____ _____

◇ PRACTICE 7. Using WHO. (Chart 9-3)
   Directions: Make questions with *who*.

1. Ron helped Judy.

   a.   _Who helped Judy?_   Ron.

   b.   _Who did Ron help?_   Judy.

2. The doctor examined the patient.

   a.   _____   The patient.

   b.   _____   The doctor.

3. Miriam called the supervisor.

   a.   _____   Miriam.

   b.   _____   The supervisor.

4. The students surprised the teacher.

   a.   _____   The students.

   b.   _____   The teacher.

5. Andrew and Catherine waited for Mrs. Allen.

   a.   _____   Mrs. Allen.

   b.   _____   Andrew and Catherine.

◇ PRACTICE 8. Using WHO. (Chart 9-3)
   Directions: Make questions with *who*.

1. A: _Who did you see?_ _____
   B: Ken. (I saw Ken.)

2. A: _____
   B: Ken. (I talked to Ken.)

3. A: _____
   B: Nancy. (I visited Nancy.)

4. A: _____
   B: Ahmed. (Ahmed answered the question.)

5. A: _____
   B: Mr. Lee. (Mr. Lee taught the English class.)

6. A: _____
   B: Carlos. (Carlos helped me.)

7. A: _____
   B. Gina. (I helped Gina.)

8. A: _____
   B: My brother. (My brother carried my suitcase.)

9. A: _____
   B: Yuko. (Yuko called.)

◇ **PRACTICE 9. Using WHO. (Chart 9-3)**
   Directions: There were some parties last week. Write questions and answers using the words in the list.

   Questions: Who gave a/an . . . party?
                  Who did . . . give a party for?

This host*	gave this party	for these people.
Ray	*anniversary party*	*his parents*
Mrs. Adams	*birthday party*	*her son*
Dr. Martin	*New Year's party*	*his employees*
Professor Brown	*graduation party*	*her students*

1. ___*Who gave an anniversay party?*___ Ray. ___*Ray gave an anniversary party.*___

2. ___*Who did Ray give a party for?*___ His parents. ___*He gave a party for his parents.*___

3. _____ Dr. Martin. _____

4. _____ Her students. _____

5. _____ Mrs. Adams. _____

6. _____ Professor Brown. _____

7. _____ His employees. _____

8. _____ Her son. _____

_____

*host = a person who entertains guests.

◇ **PRACTICE 10. Irregular verbs: Group 5. (Chart 9-4)**
Directions: Check (✓) the sentences that are true for you. Write the present form for each verb in *italics*.

PRESENT FORM

1. _____ I *forgot* to do my homework last week.   _____*forget*_____

2. _____ My teacher *gave* me extra work last week.   _____

3. _____ I *understood* my teacher on the first day of class.   _____

4. _____ I *hurt* my back last year.   _____

5. _____ I *spent* money on snack food yesterday.   _____

6. _____ Ice-cream cones *cost* a lot when I was a child.   _____

7. _____ I *lent* some money to a friend last year.   _____

8. _____ I *cut* something with a sharp knife yesterday.   _____

9. _____ I once *hit* my finger with a hammer.   _____

10. _____ I *made* only one mistake on my last grammar test.   _____

11. _____ When I was young, I *shut* a door on my finger.   _____

◇ **PRACTICE 11. Irregular verbs: Group 5. (Chart 9-4)**
Directions: Complete each sentence with the past tense form of the verb from the list. In some sentences, more than one verb is correct. The number in parentheses tells you how many verbs you can use.

cost	forget	hit	lend	✓ shut	spend
cut	give	hurt	make	understand	

Jonathan had a bad day yesterday.

1. He woke up early because there was a barking dog outside. He _____*shut*_____ his bedroom window too hard and cracked the glass. (1)

2. He _____ to bring his homework to class. His teacher wasn't happy. (1)

3. He _____ a lot of mistakes on his math quiz. (1)

4. His teacher _____ him a low grade on his research paper. (1)

5. He thought he _____ the research assignment, but his teacher said he did it wrong. (1)

6. He broke a glass container in chemistry class. When he

   picked up the glass, he _____ his hand. (2)

7. He left his lunch at home, so he bought food in the cafeteria.

   It _____ a lot. He had no money

   left. (1)

8. Because he _____ all his money, he had

   no money for the bus. (1)

9. A friend _____ him some bus money, but he lost it. (2)

10. During lunch, he played soccer with his friends. Someone kicked the ball, and it

    _____ him in the face. (2)

11. He couldn't open his eye, and his face _____ the rest of the day. (1)

◇ PRACTICE 12. Irregular verbs: Group 6. (Chart 9-5)
   Directions: Check (✓) the sentences that are true for you. Write the present form for each verb
   in *italics*.

                                                                    PRESENT FORM

   1. _____ I *knew* all the answers in the last exercise.   ___*know*___

   2. _____ I *felt* happy all day yesterday.   _____

   3. _____ When I was a child, I *kept* animals for pets.   _____

   4. _____ I *swam* in a pool last month.   _____

   5. _____ I *threw* away some homework yesterday.   _____

   6. _____ I *drew* pictures in my grammar book yesterday.   _____

   7. _____ I *grew* vegetables last summer.   _____

   8. _____ I often *fell* down when I was a child.   _____

   9. _____ I *won* a prize when I was a child.   _____

   10. _____ I *blew* bubbles with bubble gum yesterday.   _____

bubble

Expressing Past Time, Part 2 **135**

◇ **PRACTICE 13. Irregular verbs: Group 6. (Chart 9-5)**
   Directions: Complete the sentences with the past tense form of the verbs from the list. There is only one correct verb for each sentence.

✓blow	fall	grow	know	throw
draw	feel	keep	swim	won

A CRAZY DAY IN THE CLASSROOM

1. Every time the teacher spoke, she _____blew_____ a whistle.

2. Some students _____ funny pictures on the ceiling.

3. It was a hot, sunny day. Snow _____ outside the classroom.

4. The students _____ happy when they heard there was a test.
   They cheered.

5. The teacher didn't want her lesson plans. She _____ them in the
   garbage can.

6. Flowers _____ on the teacher's desk. They smelled wonderful.

7. One student _____ a pet mouse in a box on her desk.

8. A goldfish _____ upside down in the fish bowl.

9. The class played a game. The teacher asked questions, but no one _____
   the answers.

10. Both teams _____ a prize.

◇ **PRACTICE 14. Irregular verbs: Group 7. (Chart 9-6)**
Directions: Check (✓) the sentences that are true for you. Write the present form for each verb in *italics*.

		PRESENT FORM
1. _____	I once *held* a big spider in my hand.	*hold*
2. _____	I once *bent* an iron bar.	
3. _____	I *shook* the hand of a famous person once.	
4. _____	I *became* friends with a famous person.	
5. _____	I *fed* a pet (dog, cat, fish, etc.) last week.	
6. _____	When I was a baby, I *bit* people.	
7. _____	I once *hid* some keys and later couldn't find them.	
8. _____	I sometimes *fought* with my friends when I was young.	
9. _____	When I was a child, I *built* sand castles at the beach.	

sand castle

◇ **PRACTICE 15. Irregular verbs: Group 7. (Chart 9-6)**
Directions: Complete the sentences with the past tense form of the verbs from the list. In some sentences, more than one verb fits. The number in parentheses tells you how many verbs you can use.

become	*bite*	*feed*	*hide*	*shake*
bend	*build*	*fight*	*held*	

PUPPY TROUBLE

Thomas got a new puppy. He's having trouble with her. Here's what happened last week.

1. He _____*built*_____ a dog house for her, but she didn't want to sleep outdoors.

   She wanted to be inside. (1)

2. She likes to play in the rain. Yesterday, she got all wet. Then she came inside and

   _____. She got Thomas all wet. (1)

3. Thomas _____ her dog food, but she didn't eat it. She only

   wanted meat. (1)

4. He gave her dog toys, but she _____ the toys. He can't find them. (1)

5. The puppy likes to play with people. On Monday, she got excited and

   _____ the mail carrier's pant leg. Fortunately, her teeth didn't touch

   the skin. (3)

6. The mail carrier didn't understand and _____ upset. (1)

7. Thomas's big cat, Snow, doesn't like the puppy. Snow jumps at her and

   tries to scratch her. All last week, they _____. (1)

8. Thomas didn't want the puppy to get hurt. He

   _____ her in his arms a lot. (1)

9. The puppy likes to chew. She chewed Thomas's glasses.

   She _____ the frames, and now they are

   crooked. (2)

◇ PRACTICE 16. Complete and incomplete sentences. (Chart 9-7)
   Directions: Write the phrases or sentences in the correct column. Add capitalization and
   punctuation where necessary.

✓ we slept	before school starts
✓ at the store	before school starts, I help the teacher
they left	we ate at a restaurant
after they left	after we finish dinner
after several minutes	we were at home

INCOMPLETE	COMPLETE
at the store	*We slept.*

◇ **PRACTICE 17. BEFORE/AFTER.** (Chart 9-7)

Directions: Look at the pairs of sentences. Decide which action is first and which is second. Then write sentences with **before** and **after**. Pay special attention to the punctuation.

1. __1__ My computer crashed.

   __2__ I lost my information.

   After my computer crashed, I lost my information. _____ OR

   I lost my information after my computer crashed. _____

2. _____ I closed the freezer door.

   _____ I looked in the freezer.

   _____ OR

   _____

3. _____ I stood on the scale.

   _____ The nurse wrote down my weight.

   _____ OR

   _____

4. _____ I exercised.

   _____ I put on my exercise clothes.

   _____ OR

   _____

5. _____ The snow began to melt.

   _____ The sun came out.

   _____ OR

   _____

◇ **PRACTICE 18. BEFORE/AFTER.** (Chart 9-7)

Directions: Look at the pairs of sentences. Decide which action is first and which is second. Then circle the two sentences that have the same meaning.

1. __1__ Joan washed the dishes.

   __2__ Joan dried the dishes.

   (a.) After Joan washed the dishes, she dried them.

   b. Before Joan washed the dishes, she dried them.

   c. After Joan dried the dishes, she washed them.

   (d.) Before Joan dried the dishes, she washed them.

2. _____ It rained.

   _____ The rain clouds came.

   a. After it rained, the rain clouds came.

   b. Before it rained, the rain clouds came.

   c. After the rain clouds came, it rained.

   d. Before the rain clouds came, it rained.

3. _____ Luis drove away.

   _____ Luis started the car.

   a. Before Luis drove away, he started the car.

   b. Before Luis started the car, he drove away.

   c. After Luis drove away, he started the car.

   d. After Luis started the car, he drove away.

4. _____ I opened my eyes.

   _____ I looked around the room.

   a. Before I opened my eyes, I looked around the room.

   b. After I opened my eyes, I looked around the room.

   c. Before I looked around the room, I opened my eyes.

   d. After I looked around the room, I opened my eyes.

◇ PRACTICE 19. WHEN in questions and time clauses. (Chart 9-8)
   Directions: In each of the following pairs, one is a question and one is a time clause. Add the necessary punctuation: question mark or comma.

   1. a. When you called**,**

      b. When did you call**?**

   2. a. When did the movie start

      b. When the movie started

   3. a. When you were in high school

      b. When were you in high school

   4. a. When it snowed

      b. When did it snow

   5. a. When was Dave sick

      b. When Dave was sick

◇ **PRACTICE 20. WHEN in questions and time clauses. (Chart 9-8)**

Directions: Add punctuation: question mark or comma. Then make the time clause a complete sentence by adding another clause from the list.

> we felt sad.
> everyone clapped.
> ✓ I met them at the airport.
> we were happy to see you.
> the class had a test.

1. When was the Smith's party**?**

2. When the Browns came**,** *I met them at the airport.*

3. When did you hear the good news

4. When Mr. King died

5. When were you here

6. When did we meet

7. When you arrived

8. When Kevin was absent

9. When the movie ended

10. When was Mrs. Allen a teacher

◇ **PRACTICE 21. WHEN in questions and time clauses. (Chart 9-8)**

Directions: Use the given words to make (a) a past tense question and (b) a past tense clause. Then use your own words to complete the sentence in (b).

1. when \ rain \ it

   a. _____ *When did it rain?* _____

   b. _____ *When it rained, I went inside.* _____

2. when \ get sick \ you

   a. _____

   b. _____

3. when \ begin \ the movie

    a. _____

    b. _____

4. when \ visit \ they

    a. _____

    b. _____

◇ **PRACTICE 22. Forms of the past progressive.** (Chart 9-9)
Directions: Create your own chart by completing the sentences with **study** and the correct form of the past progressive.

  1. I   *was studying.* _____

  2. You   _____

  3. He   _____

  4. She   _____

  5. Ray and I   _____

  6. Several students _____

  7. We (not)   _____

  8. My children (not) _____

  9. Dr. Roberts (not) _____

10. My friends and I (not) _____

11. Your friends (not) _____

12. I (not)   _____

◇ **PRACTICE 23. Forms of the present and past progressive.** (Chart 9-9)
Directions: Complete the sentences. Use a form of **be + sit**.

  1. I ___*am sitting*___ in class right now.

  2. I ___*was sitting*___ in class yesterday too.

  3. You _____ in class right now.

  4. You _____ in class yesterday too.

  5. Tony _____ in class right now.

6. He _____ in class yesterday too.

7. We _____ in class today.

8. We _____ in class yesterday too.

9. Rita _____ in class now.

10. She _____ in class yesterday too.

11. Rita and Tony _____ in class today.

12. They _____ in class yesterday too.

◇ **PRACTICE 24. WHILE + past progressive. (Chart 9-10)**

Directions: Combine the sentences and add the correct punctuation. Use *while*.

1. We felt an earthquake.
   We were sitting in our living room last night.

   a. _____ *We felt an earthquake while we were sitting in our living room last night.*

   b. _____ *While we were sitting in our living room last night, we felt an earthquake.*

2. I was talking to the teacher yesterday.
   Another student interrupted me.

   a. _____

   b. _____

3. I was planting flowers in the garden.
   My dog began to bark at a squirrel.

   a. _____

   b. _____

4. A police officer stopped another driver for speeding.
   We were driving to work.

   a. _____

   b. _____

5. I was walking in the forest.
   A dead tree fell over.

   a. _____

   b. _____

◇ **PRACTICE 25. WHILE + past progressive. (Chart 9-10)**
   Directions: Complete each sentence with the correct form of the verb.

While Tom *(drive)* _____*was driving*_____ down the road yesterday, his cell phone
                              1

(ring) _____. He *(answer, not)* _____ it because he
          2   3

(want) _____ to be careful. He *(notice)* _____ many drivers with
          4   5

cell phones. While he *(slow)* _____ down
                                6

to make a turn, the driver in front of him suddenly

(drive) _____ off the road into a ditch. Tom *(see)*
          7

_____ a cell phone in her hand.
   8

◇ **PRACTICE 26. WHILE + past progressive. (Chart 9-10)**
   Directions: Complete each sentence with the correct form of the verb.

A: My husband and I *(be)* _____*were*_____ at my cousin's last night. While we *(sit)*
                            1

   _____ outside in the garden after dinner, her cat *(come)*
             2

   _____ up to us with a snake in its mouth. I *(scream)* _____.
           3   4

B: What *(your cousin, do)* _____?
                            5

A: She *(yell)* _____.
                 6

B: *(your husband, do)* _____ something?
                        7

A: He *(run)* _____ to the house. While he *(run)* _____,
               8   9

   the cat *(run)* _____ after him. It was so funny. My
                   10

   cousin and I *(begin)* _____ to laugh until tears ran down our faces.
                          11

◇ **PRACTICE 27. WHILE vs. WHEN. (Chart 9-11)**
   Directions: Complete each sentence with the correct form of the verb.

   1. My roommate came home late last night. I *(sleep)* _____*was sleeping*_____ when

      she *(get)* _____ home.

   2. When Gina *(call)* _____ last night, I *(take)* _____
      a bubble bath.

   3. I *(eat)* _____ lunch with my brother when I suddenly *(remember)*

      _____ my promise to pick my cousin up at school.

   4. When the movie *(start)* _____, everyone *(become)* _____
      quiet.

5. While I *(drive)* _____ to the airport, I *(see)* _____ an accident.

6. While Joan *(exercise)* _____, a salesperson *(come)* _____ to the door.

◇ PRACTICE 28. Question review. (Chapter 9)

Directions: Make questions. Use any appropriate question word: **where, when, what time, why, who, what**.

1. A: _____*Where did Ann go?*_____
   B: To the zoo. (Ann went to the zoo.)

2. A: _____
   B: Yesterday. (Ann went to the zoo yesterday.)

3. A: _____
   B: Ann. (Ann went to the zoo yesterday.)

4. A: _____
   B: Ali. (I saw Ali.)

5. A: _____
   B: At the zoo. (I saw Ali at the zoo.)

6. A: _____
   B: Yesterday. (I saw Ali at the zoo yesterday.)

7. A: _____
   B: Because the weather was nice. (I went to the zoo yesterday because the weather was nice.)

8. A: _____
   B: The doctor's office. (The doctor's office called.)

9. A: _____
   B: Yesterday afternoon. (They called yesterday afternoon.)

10. A: _____
    B: The nurse. (I talked to the nurse.)

11. A: _____
    B: At home. (I was at home yesterday afternoon.)

12. A: _____
    B: "Very old." (*Ancient* means "very old.")

13. A: _____
    B: In an apartment. (I'm living in an apartment.)

14. A: _____
    B: Grammar. (The teacher is talking about grammar.)

15. A: _____
    B: A frog. (Annie has a frog in her pocket.)

◇ **PRACTICE 29. Question review. (Chapter 9)**
   Directions: Make questions for the given answers.

1. _When did you get up this morning? / What time does the movie start? / Etc._ At 7:00.

2. _____ In an apartment.

3. _____ Yesterday.

4. _____ It means "wonderful."

5. _____ At 7:30.

6. _____ A shirt.

7. _____ Some chicken.

8. _____ No, I didn't.

9. _____ Because I wanted to.

10. _____ Grammar.

11. _____ Yes, I did.

12. _____ Nothing.

13. _____ In the dormitory.

14. _____ Because I was tired.

15. _____ Last night.

◇ **PRACTICE 30. Review: irregular verbs. (Chapters 8 and 9)**
   Directions: Choose a sentence from the list that best completes each idea.

It sold in three days.	*He ate too much for lunch.*
Someone stole his wallet.	*I caught a taxi.*
She hung up after midnight.	*She caught a cold yesterday.*
✓*He said they were too noisy.*	*Several students came to class without their homework.*
It tore when she played outside.	*I grew up there.*
Sam bent over and picked it up for her.	*She found it on the teacher's desk.*

1. The teacher told the students to work more quietly. _____He said they were too noisy._____

2. Laurie doesn't feel good. _____

3. Beth lost her grammar book. _____

4. Jack had no money. _____

5. Peter didn't want dinner. _____

6. Susan didn't want to sell her car, but she needed money. _____

_____

7. Maria wore her best dress to school. _____

_____

8. Shelley's phone conversation began at 9:00 P.M. _____

_____

9. Kathy dropped her pen on the floor. _____

_____

10. I missed the bus for the airport yesterday. _____

11. The teacher was unhappy. _____

12. My hometown is Ames, Iowa. _____

◇ **PRACTICE 31. Review: irregular verbs. (Chapters 8 and 9)**
Directions: Complete the sentences. Use the past form of the verbs in the list.

make	know	wear	fall	steal	✓throw
break	cost	meet	lose	tell	spend

1. The baseball player _____ *threw* _____ the ball to the catcher.

2. Rick _____ his arm when he fell on the ice.

3. Maggie didn't tell a lie. She _____ the truth.

4. We _____ a lot of money at the restaurant last night. The food was good, but expensive.

5. I wrote a check yesterday. I _____ a mistake on the check, so I tore it up and wrote another one.

6. I _____ my winter jacket yesterday because the weather was cold.

7. Tom bought a new tie. It _____ a lot because it was a hand-painted silk tie.

8. Leo read the story easily. The words in the story weren't new for him. He _____ the vocabulary in the story.

9. I know Amanda Clark. I _____ her at a party a couple of weeks ago.

10. I dropped my book. It _____ to the floor.

11. Jack couldn't get into his apartment because he _____ his keys.

12. Someone _____ my bicycle, so I called the police.

◇ **PRACTICE 32. Review: irregular verbs. (Chapters 8 and 9)**
   Directions: Complete the sentences. Use the past form of the verbs in the list.

✓begin	feed	fly	put	sing
build	fight	leave	shake	win

1. We were late for the movie. It _____*began*_____ at 7:00, but we didn't get there

   until 7:15.

2. We _____ songs at the party last night and had a good time.

3. I _____ to Chicago last week. The plane was only five minutes late.

4. My plane _____ at 6:03 and arrived at 8:45.

5. We played a soccer game yesterday. The other team _____. We lost.

6. When I asked Dennis a question, he _____ his head no.

7. My daughter _____ a table in her woodworking class in high school.

8. Mike stole a spoon from the restaurant. He _____ it in his pocket

   before he walked out of the restaurant.

9. The two children wanted the same toy. They _____ for a few

   minutes. Then they decided to share it.

10. Diane is a computer programmer. Yesterday she _____ information

    into the computer.

◇ **PRACTICE 33. Review: past tense. (Chapters 8 and 9)**
  Directions: Complete the sentences with the past tense of the words in parentheses.

PART I.

Yesterday *(be)* _____was_____ a terrible day. Everything *(go)*
                                1

_____ wrong. First, I *(oversleep)* _____ . My alarm
         2   3

clock *(ring, not)* _____ . I *(wake)* _____ up when I
                         4   5

(hear) _____ some noise outside my window. It was 9:15. I *(get)*
                 6

_____ dressed quickly. I *(run)* _____ to class, but I
         7   8

(be) _____ late. The teacher *(be)* _____ upset.
               9   10

PART II.

After my classes in the morning, I *(go)* _____ to the cafeteria for
                                                11

lunch. I *(have)* _____ an embarrassing accident at the cafeteria. I
                       12

accidentally *(drop)* _____ my tray of food. Some of the dishes *(break)*
                          13

_____ . When I *(drop)* _____ the tray, everyone in the
         14   15

cafeteria *(look)* _____ at me. I *(go)* _____ back to the
                       16   17

cafeteria line and *(get)* _____ a second tray of food. I *(pay)*
                               18

_____ for my lunch again. After I *(sit)* _____ down at a
         19   20

table in the corner by myself, I *(eat)* _____ my sandwich and *(drink)*
                                             21

_____ a cup of tea.
         22

PART III.

After lunch, I *(go)* _____ outside. I *(sit)* _____
23 24

under a tree near the classroom building. I *(see)* _____ a friend. I *(call)*
25

_____ to him. He *(join)* _____ me on the grass. We
26 27

(talk) _____ about our classes and *(relax)* _____ .
28 29

Everything was fine. But when I *(stand)* _____ up, I *(step)*
30

_____ in a hole and *(break)* _____ my ankle.
31 32

PART IV.

My friend *(drive)* _____ me to the hospital. We *(go)* _____
33 34

to the emergency ward. After the doctor *(take)* _____ X-rays of my ankle,
35

he *(put)* _____ a cast on it.
36

I *(pay)* _____ my bill. Then we *(leave)* _____ the
37 38

hospital. My friend *(take)* _____ me home and *(help)* _____
39 40

me up the stairs to my apartment.

PART V.

When we *(get)* _____ to the door of my apartment, I *(look)*
                       41

_____ for my key in my purse and in my pockets. There was no key. I
        42

(ring) _____ the doorbell. I *(think)* _____ that my
                 43   44

roommate might be at home, but she *(be, not)* _____ . So I *(sit)*
                                                        45

_____ down on the floor outside my apartment and *(wait)*
        46

_____ for my roommate to get home.
        47

Finally, my roommate *(come)* _____ home and I *(get)*
                                       48

_____ into the apartment. I *(eat)* _____ dinner quickly
        49   50

and *(go)* _____ to bed. I *(sleep)* _____ for ten hours. I
                 51   52

hope today is a better day than yesterday!

CHAPTER *10*
Expressing Future Time, Part 1

◇ PRACTICE 1. Forms of BE GOING TO. (Chart 10-1)

Directions: Create your own chart by completing each sentence with the correct form of *be going to*.

Don't worry.

1. I am not late.	I	*am going to be*	on time.
2. We are not late.	We	_____	on time.
3. She is not late.	She	_____	on time.
4. You are not late.	You	_____	on time.
5. They are not late.	They	_____	on time.
6. Tim and I are not late.	Tim and I	_____	on time.
7. Dr. Smith is not late.	Dr. Smith	_____	on time.
8. He is not late.	He	_____	on time.
9. Rick and Sam are not late.	Rick and Sam	_____	on time.

◇ PRACTICE 2. BE GOING TO. (Chart 10-1)

Directions: Complete each sentence with the correct form of *be going to*.

1. A: *(you, be)* ___*Are you going to be*___ at home tomorrow morning around ten?

   B: No. I *(be)* _____ out.

2. A: Where *(your roommate, go)* _____ for the summer break?

   B: She *(stay)* _____ here.

   A: Why?

   B: She *(look)* _____ for a summer job.

3. A: What (you, do) _____ tonight?

   B: I have a big test tomorrow, so I (study) _____.
      What about you?

   A: I had a big test today, so tonight I (relax) _____.

4. A: (Ed and Nancy, join) _____
      us at the restaurant for dinner?

   B: Yes, they (meet) _____ us there at 7:00.

◇ **PRACTICE 3. BE GOING TO. (Chart 10-1)**
   Directions: Complete the sentences. Use **be going to** and the given expression.

take it back	eat a big lunch	do a search on the Internet
check the lost-and-found	✓go back to bed	look for a bigger place
call the neighbors	take some medicine	

1. It's 8:00 A.M. and I'm very tired.

   I ____*am going to go back to bed.*_____

2. I'm hungry. I didn't have breakfast.

   I _____

3. I have a stomachache.

   I _____

4. The dog next door is barking loudly.

   I _____

5. Richard needs to get some information about earthquakes for a school project.

   He _____

6. The Smiths have a new baby. Their apartment is too small.

   They _____

7. Diane left her purse in the classroom.

   She _____

8. The zipper broke on my new dress.

   I _____

◇ **PRACTICE 4. BE GOING TO. (Chart 10-1)**

Directions: Read the paragraph. Rewrite the paragraph using ***be going to***.

Ricky likes to relax on his day off. Here is his schedule.

He wakes up at 9:00. He watches sports on TV for a while. Then he goes to a café for breakfast. After breakfast, he calls up his friends. They make plans for the weekend. He rents a DVD for the afternoon. Before dinner, he checks his e-mail. For dinner, he picks up fast food. Later he goes to the gym, but not for exercise. He sits next to the exercise machines with his best friend. They talk about their busy day.

Tomorrow is Ricky's day off. What is he going to do?

He is going to wake up at 9:00. _____

_____

_____

_____

_____

_____

◇ **PRACTICE 5. BE GOING TO. (Chart 10-1)**

Directions: Write answers to the question ***What are you going to do?*** Use ***be going to*** in your answers.

1. You're thirsty. ___*I am going to get a drink of water.*___

2. You have a sore throat. _____

3. You broke a tooth. _____

4. Your alarm didn't go off. You are in bed and class starts in fifteen minutes. _____

_____

5. It's midnight. You are wide awake and you want to go to sleep. _____

_____

6. You are at school. You locked your bike in a bike rack, and now it's gone. _____

_____

◇ **PRACTICE 6. BE GOING TO: negative and question forms.** **(Chart 10-1)**
   Directions: Create your own chart by rewriting the given sentences as negatives and questions.

	NEGATIVE	QUESTION
1. I am going to eat.	*I am not going to eat.*	*Am I going to eat?*
2. You are going to eat.	_____	_____
3. He is going to eat.	_____	_____
4. She is going to eat.	_____	_____
5. We are going to eat.	_____	_____
6. They are going to eat.	_____	_____
7. My friend is going to eat.	_____	_____
8. The students are going to eat.	_____	_____

◇ **PRACTICE 7. BE GOING TO.** **(Chart 10-1)**
   Directions: Complete each sentence with the correct form of the verb in parentheses. Use **be going to**.

1. A: What *(you, do)* _____ are you going to do _____ next weekend?

   B: We *(go)* _____ fishing at a lake in the mountains.

   A: *(you, stay)* _____ overnight?

   B: No. We *(come)* _____ back the same day.

2. A: Where *(Sally, work)* _____ this summer?

   B: She *(work, not)* _____. She *(take)*

   _____ summer school classes.

3. A: *(the students, have)* _____

   an end-of-the-year party?

   B: Yes, they are. They *(have)* _____ a picnic
   at the park near the beach.

4. A: *(Joan and Bob, move)* _____ next month?

   B: Yes. Joan *(start)* _____ a new job in the city.

   A: *(they, look for)* _____ a house?

   B: No, they *(look for, not)* _____ a house.

   They *(rent)* _____ an apartment.

◇ **PRACTICE 8. Using the present progressive for future time.** (Chart 10-2)
Directions: Rewrite the sentences using the present progressive for the future verbs.

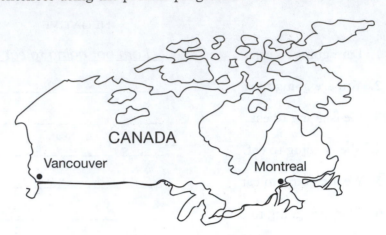

1. The Johnsons are going to take a camping trip across Canada this summer.

   The Johnsons are taking a camping trip across Canada this summer.

2. They are going to take their teenage grandchildren with them.

   _____

3. They are going to stay in parks and campgrounds.

   _____

4. They are going to leave from Vancouver in June.

   _____

5. They are going to arrive in Montreal in August.

   _____

6. Mr. and Mrs. Johnson are going to drive back home alone.

   _____

7. Their grandchildren are going to fly home because they don't want to miss the beginning

   of school.

   _____

   _____

8. Their parents are going to meet them at the airport.

   _____

◇ **PRACTICE 9. Using the present progressive for future time. (Chart 10-2)**

Directions: Write "P" if the sentence has a present meaning. Write "F" if the sentence has a future meaning.

1. ___P___ Wait! I'm coming.

2. _____ I'm coming at 8:00 tonight.

3. _____ You're leaving in the morning.

4. _____ Ron is taking us to the airport soon.

5. _____ Claude and Marie are spending their next vacation hiking in the mountains.

6. _____ I'm returning this library book. I'm sorry it's late.

7. _____ We're flying to Rome in a few weeks.

8. _____ Joe, are you leaving?

9. _____ I'm not going. I'm staying.

◇ **PRACTICE 10. Using YESTERDAY, LAST, TOMORROW, NEXT, IN, or AGO. (Chart 10-3)**

Directions: Complete the sentences. Use *yesterday, last, tomorrow, next, in,* or *ago.*

1. I went to Hawaii _____*last*_____ year.

2. I went to Hawaii a year _____.

3. My sister went to Hawaii a week _____.

4. My sister went to Hawaii _____ week.

5. Our neighbors are going to Hawaii _____ Friday.

6. We're going to Hawaii _____ two weeks.

7. My parents went to Hawaii _____ afternoon.

8. Their friends are going to Hawaii _____ morning.

9. My cousins are going to Hawaii _____ three weeks.

10. Were you home _____ afternoon around 4:00?

11. Were you home _____ night around 9:00?

12. Are you going to be home _____ afternoon around 3:00?

13. I wasn't at work two days _____.

14. I'm not going to be at work _____ Thursday.

◇ PRACTICE 11. Using A COUPLE OF with past and future. (Chart 10-4)
   Directions: Check (✓) the expressions that can mean *a couple of*. Rewrite the expressions using *a couple of*.

   1. _____ seven minutes _____

   2. __✓__ two hours ___*a couple of hours*_____

   3. _____ five days _____

   4. _____ six years _____

   5. _____ three months _____

   6. _____ two years _____

   7. _____ four hours _____

   8. _____ one minute _____

   9. _____ two weeks _____

◇ PRACTICE 12. Using A FEW with past and future. (Chart 10-4)
   Directions: Check (✓) the expressions that can mean *a few*. Rewrite the expressions using *a few*.

   1. __✓__ five minutes ___*a few minutes*_____

   2. _____ seven months _____

   3. _____ four hours _____

   4. _____ three days _____

   5. _____ ten weeks _____

   6. _____ five years _____

   7. _____ one day _____

◇ PRACTICE 13. Using A COUPLE OF/A FEW with past and future. (Chart 10-4)
   Directions: Make sentences using the given words.

   1. I \ leave

      a. *(in a few days)*

         ___*I am going to leave in a few days.*_____

      b. *(a few days ago)*

         ___*I left a few days ago.*_____

2. Susie \ marry Paul

   a. *(in a couple of months)*

   _____

   b. *(a couple of months ago)*

   _____

3. Dr. Nelson \ retire

   a. *(a few years ago)*

   _____

   b. *(in a few years)*

   _____

4. Jack \ begin a new job

   a. *(a couple of days ago)*

   _____

   b. *(in a couple of days)*

   _____

◇ **PRACTICE 14. Using THIS with time words and TODAY/TONIGHT. (Chart 10-5)**
   Directions: Circle the meaning of each sentence: past, present, or future time.

1. Tom is going to finish school this June.	past	present	(future)
2. We took my parents to the airport this morning.	past	present	future
3. Nancy is at her grandmother's. She is cleaning her house this morning.	past	present	future
4. Mrs. Andrew had lunch with friends today.	past	present	future
5. Our secretary is going to retire this month.	past	present	future
6. The children are studying dinosaurs this month.	past	present	future
7. I am doing a lot of work today.	past	present	future
8. We heard about an interesting movie this morning.	past	present	future
9. You are going to have a good time today.	past	present	future
10. I had fun this evening.	past	present	future
11. Are you going to be home this afternoon?	past	present	future

◇ PRACTICE 15. Using THIS with time words. (Chart 10-5)
Directions: Read the story about Sara. Then answer the questions.

Right now, I'm sitting in my kitchen. I'm thinking about going to school. This morning I woke up late. I looked at the alarm clock. It was very late, and I missed my math class. I have an important chemistry test this afternoon. I have a problem. I don't want to miss it, but my chemistry teacher is also my math teacher. I'm not sure what to do. I'm going to sit at the kitchen table and think about a solution.

1. What are two things Sara did this morning?

   a. _____She woke up late._____

   b. _____

2. What are two things Sara is going to do this morning?

   a. _____

   b. _____

3. What is one thing Sara is doing this morning?

   _____

◇ PRACTICE 16. Using TODAY and THIS + time words. (Chart 10-5)
Directions: Read the description of Sophia's morning. Then circle the correct answer.

It's 6:00 A.M. Sophia is brushing her teeth. Then she is going to get dressed, have breakfast, and go to school.

1. What is true about Sophia's morning?
   a. She woke up early this morning.
   b. She is going to wake up early this morning.
   c. She is waking up early this morning.

2. What is also true about her morning?
   a. Sophia went to school this morning.
   b. Sophia is going to go to school this morning.
   c. Sophia is going to school right now.

3. Where is Sophia this morning?
   a. She is in the bathroom.
   b. She was in the bathroom.
   c. She is going to be in the bathroom.

◇ PRACTICE 17. Forms of WILL. (Chart 10-6)
Directions: Create your own chart by completing the sentences with the correct forms of **will**.

1. We aren't late.   We   _____will be_____ there soon.

2. You aren't late.   You   _____ there soon.

3. They aren't late.   They _____ there soon.

4. She isn't late.   She _____ there soon.

5. I'm not late.   I _____ there soon.

6. The students aren't late.   The students _____ there soon.

7. My mother isn't late.   My mother _____ there soon.

8. He isn't late.   He _____ there soon.

9. Jill and I aren't late.   Jill and I _____ there soon.

10. Eva and her son
aren't late.   Eva and her son _____ there soon.

◇ PRACTICE 18. WILL. (Chart 10-6)

Directions: Imagine you are a tourist in Paris. What are you going to do? Complete the sentences with *will* or *won't*.

1. I _____ ride to the top of the Eiffel Tower.

2. I _____ eat pastries in a French café.

3. I _____ speak French.

4. I _____ speak my own language.

5. I _____ go shopping in expensive shops.

6. I _____ ride the subway.

7. I _____ visit famous museums.

8. I _____ try on French perfume.

9. I _____ take a tour of Paris.

10. I _____ eat dinner in a five-star restaurant.

◇ PRACTICE 19. WILL. (Chart 10-6)

Directions: What will happen fifty years from now? Complete the sentences with *will* or *won't* and the words in parentheses.

Fifty years from now . . .

1. most people *(live)* _____ to be 100.

2. people *(travel)* _____ to other planets.

3. computers *(be)* _____ the size of cell phones.

4. students *(study)* _____ at home with computers, not at school.

5. students (*study*) _____ in the classroom.

6. some people (*live*) _____ in underwater homes.

7. scientists (*discover*) _____ cures for serious diseases like cancer and AIDS.

8. there (*be*) _____ wars.

9. the world (*be*) _____ peaceful.

◇ PRACTICE 20. WILL. (Chart 10-6)
Directions: Change the sentences by using *will* to express future time.

1. Class is going to finish a few minutes early today.
   Class will finish a few minutes early today.

2. I am going to pick you up after school.
   _____

3. Hurry or we aren't going to be on time for the movie.
   _____

4. Your brother and sister are going to help you with your science project.
   _____

5. The bus isn't going to be on time today.
   _____

6. Watch out! You're going to cut yourself with that sharp knife.
   _____

7. Carlos and Olivia are going to graduate from nursing school next year.
   _____

◇ PRACTICE 21. Forms of BE GOING TO and WILL. (Charts 10-5 → 10-7)
Directions: Complete each sentence with the correct form of the verb.

BE GOING TO + GO	WILL + GO
1. I ___am going to go___.	I ___will go___.
2. You _____.	You _____.
3. The students _____.	The students _____.
4. Ms. Jenkins _____.	Ms. Jenkins _____.
5. Our friends _____.	Our friends _____.

Negative

6. Mr. Davis *(not)* _____.   Mr. Davis *(not)* _____.

7. I *(not)* _____.   I *(not)* _____.

8. We *(not)* _____.   We *(not)* _____.

Question

9. *(she, go)* _____?   *(she, go)* _____?

10. *(they, go)* _____?   *(they, go)* _____?

11. *(you, go)* _____?   *(you, go)* _____?

◇ **PRACTICE 22. Questions with WILL. (Chart 10-7)**

Directions: Make questions using the given words.

In the future . . .

1. you \ live to be 100 years old?

    Will you live to be 100 years old? _____

2. your friends \ live to be 100 years old?

    _____

3. your children \ live to be 100 years old?

    _____

4. we \ live on another planet?

    _____

5. my friends \ live on another planet?

    _____

6. some people \ live underwater?

    _____

7. I \ live underwater?

    _____

8. countries \ find a solution for poverty?

    _____

◇ **PRACTICE 23. Questions with WILL. (Chart 10-7)**

Directions: Read the story about Frank. Write questions with ***will***. Then give short answers using ***will*** or ***won't***.

      Frank is a lazy student. He is not passing his classes. Beginning Monday, he is going to change his behavior. He is going to do his homework every night. He isn't going to forget to bring his homework to class. He isn't going to stay up late on weeknights. He is going to go to bed early and get a good night's sleep. He is going to stop going to parties on weekends. He is also going to stop eating junk food, and instead eat lots of fruits and vegetables because he wants to have more energy. He is going to exercise every day after he gets home from school. Frank knows he is going to feel better and do better in school.

1. change his behavior

     Will he change his behavior?   Yes, he will.

2. do his homework every night

3. forget to bring his homework to school

4. go to parties on weekends

5. eat junk food

6. eat healthy food

7. exercise often

8. be a better student

◇ **PRACTICE 24. Verb review: present, past, and future. (Chart 10-8)**
   Directions: Make questions with the given words.

   1. you \ need \ help \ now?

      _____Do you need help now?_____

   2. you \ need \ help \ tomorrow?

      _____

   3. you \ need \ help \ yesterday?

      _____

   4. Eva \ need \ help \ yesterday?

      _____

   5. Eva \ need \ help \ tomorrow?

      _____

   6. Eva \ need \ help \ now?

      _____

   7. the students \ need \ help \ now?

      _____

   8. the students \ need \ help \ tomorrow?

      _____

   9. the students \ need \ help \ yesterday?

      _____

◇ **PRACTICE 25. Verb review: present, past, and future. (Chart 10-8)**
   Directions: Complete each sentence with the correct form of the verb in parentheses.

   1. Right now, Becky *(eat)* _____is eating_____ fish for lunch.

   2. She *(eat)* _____ fish for lunch once or twice a week.

   3. She also *(eat)* _____ chicken often.

   4. She *(eat)* _____ chicken for dinner several times last week.

   5. Last night Becky *(cook)* _____ a spicy chicken and rice dish for
      her friends.

   6. It *(be)* _____ delicious, and they *(love)* _____ it.

7. While she was cooking dinner, she *(drop)* _____ a pan

of hot oil on the floor, but fortunately she *(be)* _____ okay.

It *(burn, not)* _____ her.

8. Tomorrow Becky *(have)* _____ her parents over for lunch.

9. *(she, cook)* _____ fish?

10. *(she, fix)* _____ chicken?

11. Maybe she *(prepare, not)* _____ chicken or fish.

12. Maybe she *(surprise)* _____ her parents with a completely new dish.

◇ **PRACTICE 26. Verb review: BE. (Chart 10-9)**
   Directions: Make sentences with the given words.

1. you \ be \ sick \ now?

   _____*Are you sick now?*_____

2. you \ be \ sick \ tomorrow?

   _____

3. you \ be \ sick \ yesterday?

   _____

4. Steve \ be \ sick \ yesterday?

   _____

5. Steve \ be \ sick \ tomorrow?

   _____

6. Steve \ be \ sick \ now?

   _____

7. the children \ be \ sick \ now?

   _____

8. the children \ be \ sick \ tomorrow?

   _____

9. the children \ be \ sick \ yesterday?

   _____

◇ **PRACTICE 27. Verb review: BE.** (Chart 10-9)

Directions: Complete each sentence with the correct form of the verb in parentheses.

1. I *(be)* _____ am _____ very busy today. Right now, I *(be)* _____ in

   Quebec. Tomorrow I *(be)* _____ in New York. Yesterday

   I *(be)* _____ in Paris. I *(be)* _____ home next week.

2. A: Where *(you, be)* _____ last night? *(you, be)*

   _____ at home?

   B: No, I *(be, not)* _____. I *(be)* _____ at the library with my friends.

   A: I *(be)* _____ there too. Where *(you, be)* _____?

   B: We *(be)* _____ in the study area.

   A: Oh. I *(be)* _____ in the reference section.

3. A: *(a dolphin, be)* _____ a fish?

   B: No, it *(be, not)* _____. It *(be)* _____ a mammal.

   A: What about sharks? *(they, be)* _____ mammals?

   B: No, they *(be, not)* _____. They *(be)* _____ fish.

   A: I like learning about fish. Tomorrow our class is going to the aquarium. *(you, be)*

   _____ there?

   B: Yes, I *(be)* _____ there too.

◇ **PRACTICE 28. Simple present questions.** (Charts 10-8 and 10-9)

Directions: Complete the sentences with *are* or *do*.

Jane is going to a new high school this morning. Her mother is asking her questions.

1. _____ Do _____ you want to get there early?

2. _____ you have your books?

3. _____ you excited?

4. _____ you know your teachers' names?

5. _____ you a little scared?

6. _____ you need lunch money?

7. _____ you ready to go?

8. _____ you okay?

9. _____ you want me to be quiet?

◇ PRACTICE 29. Simple past questions. (Charts 10-8 and 10-9)
    Directions: Complete the sentences with *were* or *did*.

Dan had an important math test this morning. A friend is asking him about it.

1. _____*Did*_____ you study for the test last night?

2. _____ you get enough sleep?

3. _____ you nervous this morning?

4. _____ you ready for the test?

5. _____ you do well?

6. _____ you make any mistakes?

7. _____ you get 100%?

8. _____ you happy when you finished?

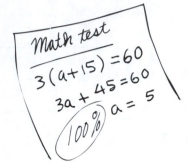

◇ PRACTICE 30. Verb review: present, past, and future. (Charts 10-8 and 10-9)
    Directions: Complete the chart with the correct forms of the verbs.

EVERY DAY/NOW	YESTERDAY	TOMORROW
1. I **drink** tea every day. I ___*am drinking*___ tea now.	I _____*drank*_____ tea yesterday.	I ___*am going to drink*___ tea tomorrow. I _____*will drink*_____ tea tomorrow.
2. We **work** every day. We _____ now.	I _____ yesterday.	I _____ tomorrow. I _____ tomorrow.
3. She **is** late every day. She _____ late now.	She _____ late yesterday.	She _____ late tomorrow. She _____ late tomorrow.
4. You _____ me every day. You _____ me now.	You **helped** me yesterday.	You _____ me tomorrow. You _____ me tomorrow.
5. She **doesn't come** every day. She _____ now.	She _____ yesterday.	She _____ tomorrow. She _____ tomorrow.

EVERY DAY/NOW	YESTERDAY	TOMORROW
6. She _____ the dishes every day. She **isn't doing** the dishes now.	She _____ the dishes yesterday.	She _____ the dishes tomorrow. She _____ the dishes tomorrow.
7. _____ every day? **Are they exercising** now?	_____ yesterday?	_____ tomorrow? _____ tomorrow?
8. _____ on time every day? _____ on time now?	**Was he** on time yesterday?	_____ on time tomorrow? _____ on time tomorrow?
9. She _____*isn't*_____ on time every day. She _____ on time now.	She _____ on time yesterday.	She _____ on time tomorrow. She _____ on time tomorrow.

◇ PRACTICE 31. Verb review: past, present, and future.

Directions: Complete the sentences. Use the words in parentheses. Use any appropriate verb form.

1. A: I *(lose)* _____*lost*_____ my sunglasses yesterday.

   B: Where?

   A: I *(think)* _____ that I *(leave)* _____ them on a table at the restaurant.

2. A: What *(you, wear)* _____ to the party this weekend?

   B: I *(wear)* _____ my jeans. It *(be)* _____

   _____ a casual party.

3. A: Sometimes children tell little lies. You talked to Annie. *(she, tell)* _____

   the truth, or *(she, tell)* _____ a lie?

   B: She *(tell)* _____ the truth. She's honest.

4. A: How are you getting along?

   B: Fine. *(I, make)* _____ a lot of friends, and my English

   (get) _____ better.

5. A: Where *(you, go)* _____ yesterday?

   B: *(I, go)* _____ to my cousin's house. I *(see)* _____ Jean

   there and *(talk)* _____ to her for a while. And I *(meet)* _____

   my cousin's neighbors, Mr. and Mrs. Bell. They're nice people. I *(like)*

   _____ them.

6. A: What are you going to do tonight? *(you, study)* _____?

   B: No. I *(have, not)* _____ any homework.

   A: Really?

   B: Our teacher *(give)* _____ us a lot of work last week. She *(give)*

   _____ us a break this week.

7. A: *(you, do)* _____ your homework last night?

   B: No. I *(be)* _____ too tired. I *(go)* _____ to bed early and

   (sleep) _____ for nine hours.

8. A: Good morning.

   B: Excuse me?

   A: I *(say)* _____ , "Good morning."

   B: Oh! Good morning! I'm sorry. I *(understand, not)* _____

   at first.

9. A: Where *(Cathy, be)* _____? I need to talk to her.

   B: She *(meet)* _____ with some students right now.

10. I almost *(have)* _____ an accident yesterday. A dog *(run)*

   _____ into the street in front of my car. I *(slam)* _____ on my

   brakes and just *(miss)* _____ the dog.

11. Yesterday I *(play)* _____ ball with my son. He *(catch)* _____

   the ball most of the time, but sometimes he *(drop)* _____ it.

12. A: *(you, send)* _____ a birthday card to George yesterday?

   B: Oops! I *(forget)* _____ .

CHAPTER 11
Expressing Future Time, Part 2

◇ PRACTICE 1. MAY, MIGHT, WILL. (Chart 11-1)
Directions: Circle the meaning of the sentence: "sure" or "unsure."

		sure	unsure
1.	It may rain tomorrow.	sure	(unsure)
2.	I will be absent tomorrow.	sure	unsure
3.	Joe and Jeff won't be at work tomorrow.	sure	unsure
4.	We might take a trip next week.	sure	unsure
5.	Sandra may take a vacation soon.	sure	unsure
6.	Maybe we will have a picnic this weekend.	sure	unsure
7.	We won't go camping next week.	sure	unsure
8.	Our English class may get together for dinner tomorrow.	sure	unsure
9.	Some of our teachers might be there.	sure	unsure
10.	Some of our teachers won't be there.	sure	unsure

◇ PRACTICE 2. MAY, MIGHT, WILL. (Chart 11-1)
Directions: Complete the sentences with **may**, **might**, **will**, or **won't** and the verb in parentheses. Give your own opinion.

One hundred years from now, . . .

1. people (*live*) _____ longer.

2. people (*travel*) _____ easily to space.

3. drivers (*have*) _____ flying cars.

4. students (*learn*) _____ at home on their computers instead of at school.

5. people (*use*) _____ energy from the sun for electricity.

6. there (*be*) _____ enough food and water for everyone in the world.

7. all people (*speak*) _____ the same language.

8. all people (*live*) _____ in peace.

171

◇ **PRACTICE 3. MAYBE vs. MAY BE. (Chart 11-2)**
Directions: Make sentences using the given words.

1. It \ be \ sunny tomorrow

    a. *(may)* _____ *It may be sunny tomorrow.* _____

    b. *(maybe)* _____ *Maybe it will be sunny tomorrow.* _____

2. You \ need to see \ a doctor soon

    a. *(might)* _____

    b. *(maybe)* _____

3. We \ play soccer \ after school

    a. *(might)* _____

    b. *(may)* _____

4. Our class \ go \ to a movie together

    a. *(maybe)* _____

    b. *(may)* _____

◇ **PRACTICE 4. MAYBE vs. MAY BE. (Chart 11-2)**
Directions: Circle the correct sentences. In some cases, both sentences may be correct.

1. a. The teacher may gives a test tomorrow.
   b. Maybe the teacher will give a test tomorrow.

2. a. Maybe all the students do well.
   b. Maybe all the students will do well.

3. a. I may need your advice.
   b. Maybe I will need your advice.

4. a. Maybe traffic will be heavy later.
   b. Maybe traffic is heavy later.

5. a. You may will need more time.
   b. Maybe you will need more time.

6. a. We may delay our trip for a few days.
   b. Maybe we will delay our trip for a few days.

◇ **PRACTICE 5. MAY, MIGHT, and MAYBE. (Charts 11-1 and 11-2)**
Directions: Rewrite the given sentences.

TOMORROW	MAY	MIGHT
1. Maybe I will study.	*I may study.*	*I might study.*
2. Maybe they will study.		

TOMORROW	MIGHT	MAYBE
3. Maybe she won't study.	_____	_____
4. We may need help.	_____	_____
5. I may not need help.	_____	_____

	MAY	MAYBE
6. He might understand.	_____	_____
7. You might understand.	_____	_____
8. They might not understand.	_____	_____

◇ PRACTICE 6. Review: MAYBE, MAY, MIGHT, and WILL. (Chart 11-2)

Directions: Make sentences with the given words and the ideas in parentheses. Use *maybe, may, might,* or *will*.

1. It \ snow \ tomorrow *(you are sure)*

   _____ *It will snow tomorrow.* _____

2. It \ snow \ next week *(you are unsure)*

   _____

3. We \ go ice-skating *(you are unsure)*

   _____

4. The children \ play in the snow *(you are sure)*

   _____

5. The snow \ melt, not \ for several days *(you are sure)*

   _____

◇ PRACTICE 7. Review: MAYBE, MAY, MIGHT, and WILL. (Chart 11-2)

Directions: Circle the letters of the correct sentences in each group. In some cases, more than one sentence may be correct.

1. (a.) Maybe I am going to skip class tomorrow.
   b. Maybe I skip class tomorrow.
   (c.) I might skip class tomorrow.
   (d.) Maybe I will skip class tomorrow.

2. a. It will snow in the mountains next week.
   b. It might snow in the mountains next week.
   c. Maybe it snows in the mountains next week.
   d. Maybe it will snow in the mountains next week.

3. a. We may not have a warm summer this year.

   b. We won't have a warm summer this year.

   c. Maybe we won't have a warm summer this year.

   d. Maybe we don't have a warm summer this year.

4. a. Maybe you be need extra time for the test tomorrow.

   b. You might need extra time for the test tomorrow.

   c. You may be need extra time for the test tomorrow.

   d. Maybe you will need extra time for the test tomorrow.

◇ PRACTICE 8. BEFORE and AFTER. (Chart 11-3)
   Directions: Look at the pairs of sentences. Decide which action is first and which is second. Then write two sentences: one with *before* and one with *after*. Use a form of *be going to* in the main clause.

1. ___1___ I boil the water.

   ___2___ I put in the rice.

   a. ____After I boil the water, I am going to put in the rice.____

   b. ____Before I put in the rice, I am going to boil the water.____

2. _____ I turn in my homework.

   _____ I check my answers one time.

   a. _____

   b. _____

3. _____ I wash the dishes.

   _____ I clear off the table.

   a. _____

   b. _____

4. _____ I put on warm clothes.

   _____ I go out in the snow.

   a. _____

   b. _____

5. _____ I board the airplane.

   _____ I go to the departure gate.

   DEPARTURES
   Gate 12

   a. _____

   b. _____

◇ PRACTICE 9. BEFORE, AFTER, and WHEN. (Chart 11-3)
   Directions: Write logical sentences with the given words.

   Carlos is a student. What is he going to do tomorrow?

   1. make breakfast \ get up

      After _____*he gets up, he is going to / will make breakfast.*_____

   2. eat breakfast \ go to school

      Before _____

   3. go to his classroom \ get to school

      After _____

   4. have lunch in the cafeteria \ talk to his friends

      When _____

   5. cook dinner for his roommates \ pick up food for dinner

      Before _____

   6. do his homework \ go to bed

      Before _____

   7. fall asleep \ have good dreams

      After _____

◇ PRACTICE 10. BEFORE, AFTER, and WHEN. (Chart 11-3)
   Directions: Complete the sentences with the words in parentheses.

   1. Before I *(fix)* _____*fix*_____ dinner tonight, I *(get)* _____*am going to get*_____ OR

      _____*will get*_____ fresh vegetables from my garden.

   2. After I *(have)* _____ dinner, I *(go)* _____ out with
      friends for dessert.

   3. When I *(see)* _____ my friends, we *(make)* _____
      plans for a camping trip this summer.

   4. Before Susan *(take)* _____ the driving test next week, she *(practice)*
      _____ with her parents.

   5. Susan *(feel)* _____ nervous when she *(take)* _____
      the test.

   6. After Susan *(get)* _____ her license, she *(be)* _____
      a careful driver.

◇ **PRACTICE 11. Clauses with IF.** (Chart 11-4)
   Directions: Complete the sentences with the correct verbs in parentheses.

   1. If Ellen *(wins, will win)* _____wins_____ a scholarship, she *(attends, will attend)* _____ a four-year college or university.

   2. If she *(goes, will go)* _____ to a college or university, she *(is going to study, studies)* _____ chemistry.

   3. If she *(enjoys, will enjoy)* _____ chemistry, she *(takes, will take)* _____ pre-med* courses.

   4. She *(applies, will apply)* _____ to medical school if she *(is going to do, does)* _____ well in her pre-med courses.

   5. If she *(will attend, attends)* _____ medical school, she *(majors in, is going to major in)* _____ family medicine.

   6. If she *(completes, is going to complete)* _____ her training, she *(works, is going to work)* _____ around the world helping people.

◇ **PRACTICE 12. Clauses with IF.** (Chart 11-4)
   Directions: Complete the sentences with the verbs in parentheses.

   1. If it *(be)* _____is_____ sunny tomorrow, Jake *(work)* _____is going to work_____ OR _____will work_____ outside in his garden.

   2. If it *(rain)* _____ tomorrow, I *(work, not)* _____ in my garden.

   3. If Beth *(get)* _____ a high score on her college entrance exams, her parents *(be)* _____ proud of her.

   4. Her parents *(get)* _____ her extra help if she *(do, not)* _____ well.

   5. If Mark *(get)* _____ a job as a tour guide this summer, he *(earn)* _____ enough money for school next year.

   6. If Mark *(get, not)* _____ a good job, he *(delay)* _____ school for a year.

   _____
   **pre-med* = classes that prepare a student for medical school.*

7. If Lesley *(feel)* _____ sick tomorrow, she *(come, not)* _____

_____ to school.

8. She *(call)* _____ you for the homework assignments if she

(miss) _____ class.

9. If Brian *(need)* _____ help this weekend, we *(help)* _____ him.

10. We *(make)* _____ other plans if he *(need, not)* _____

help next week.

◇ **PRACTICE 13. BEFORE, AFTER, and IF. (Charts 11-3 and 11-4)**
Directions: Complete the sentences with the words in parentheses.

On Ana's birthday, Alex is going to ask Ana to marry him.

He *(ask)* ___*is going to ask / will ask*___ her after they *(celebrate)*
⠀⠀⠀⠀⠀⠀⠀⠀⠀⠀⠀⠀⠀1

___*celebrate*___ her birthday at a restaurant. Before Alex
⠀⠀⠀⠀2

(talk) _____ to Ana, he *(meet)* _____ with
⠀⠀⠀⠀⠀⠀3⠀⠀⠀⠀⠀⠀⠀⠀⠀⠀⠀⠀⠀⠀⠀⠀⠀⠀⠀⠀4

her parents.

If they *(agree)* _____, Alex *(buy)* _____
⠀⠀⠀⠀⠀⠀⠀⠀⠀⠀⠀⠀⠀5⠀⠀⠀⠀⠀⠀⠀⠀⠀⠀⠀⠀⠀⠀⠀⠀⠀⠀6

an engagement ring for Ana. If Ana *(say)* _____ "yes," Alex *(give)*
⠀⠀⠀⠀⠀⠀⠀⠀⠀⠀⠀⠀⠀⠀⠀⠀⠀⠀⠀⠀⠀⠀⠀7

_____ it to her for her present. If Ana *(say, not)*
⠀⠀⠀⠀⠀8

_____ "yes," Alex *(keep)* _____ the ring and
⠀⠀⠀⠀⠀9⠀⠀⠀⠀⠀⠀⠀⠀⠀⠀⠀⠀⠀⠀⠀⠀⠀⠀⠀⠀⠀10

try again later.

◇ **PRACTICE 14. Habitual present. (Chart 11-5)**
Directions: Make sentences using the habitual present.

PART I. Match each phrase in Column A with a phrase in Column B. Write the letter in the blank.

COLUMN A	COLUMN B
1. __*F*__ drink too much coffee	A. my eyes get red
2. _____ cry	B. get home late
3. _____ not pay my electric bill	C. not answer it
4. _____ the phone rings in the middle of the night	D. get low grades on the tests
5. _____ get to work late	E. have no electricity
6. _____ have a big breakfast	✓F. feel shaky and nervous
7. _____ not do my homework	G. have a lot of energy

PART II. Now, write habitual present sentences beginning with ***If I*** . . . .

1.   <u>If I drink too much coffee, I feel shaky and nervous.</u>

2.   _____

3.   _____

4.   _____

5.   _____

6.   _____

7.   _____

◇ **PRACTICE 15. Habitual present. (Chart 11-5)**
   Directions: Answer the questions using ***if.*** Pay special attention to punctuation.

1. How do you feel if you're late for class?

   a.   <u>If I'm late for class, I feel nervous.</u>

   b.   <u>I feel nervous if I'm late for class.</u>

2. How do you feel after you eat too much?

   a. After _____

   b. _____ after _____

3. What do you do if you get a headache?

   a. If _____

   b. _____ if _____

4. What do you do when your teacher talks too fast?

   a. When _____

   b. _____ if _____

◇ **PRACTICE 16. Habitual present vs. future. (Chart 11-5)**
    Directions: Circle "present habit" or "future" for each sentence.

1. When I'm tired, I take a nap.	(present habit)	future
2. If I'm tired, I'm going to take a nap.	present habit	future
3. After the café closes, the manager will clean the kitchen.	present habit	future
4. After the café closes, the manager cleans the kitchen.	present habit	future
5. Before I get up, I listen to the news on the radio.	present habit	future
6. When Nancy moves to the city, she is going to sell her car.	present habit	future
7. Tim is going to check out of his hotel room before he has breakfast.	present habit	future
8. When Tim goes to the airport, he takes a taxi.	present habit	future
9. After Tim checks out of his hotel, he will call for a taxi.	present habit	future

◇ **PRACTICE 17. Habitual present vs. future. (Chart 11-5)**
    Directions: Complete the sentences with the words in parentheses.

1. My friends and I *(like)* _____like_____ to go swimming in the lake if the weather

    (be) _____is_____ warm.

2. We *(go)* _____ swimming tomorrow if the weather *(be)*

    _____ warm.

3. Before I *(go)* _____ to class today, I *(meet)* _____

    my friends for coffee.

4. Before I *(go)* _____ to my first class, I *(meet, usually)* _____

    my friends in the cafeteria.

5. I *(buy)* _____ some stamps when I *(go)* _____ to

    the post office this afternoon.

6. Jim *(be)* _____ often tired when he *(get)* _____ home from

    work. If he *(feel)* _____ tired, he *(exercise)* _____ for thirty

    minutes. After he *(exercise)* _____, he *(begin)* _____ to feel

    better.

7. If I *(be)* _____ tired tonight, I *(exercise, not)* _____.
I need to work late at the office tonight.

8. When Mr. and Mrs. Rose *(travel)* _____ on planes,

they *(bring)* _____ their own snacks.

9. When they *(travel)* _____ to New York next week,

they *(pack)* _____ enough food for lunch and
dinner.

10. Jane is usually on time for appointments. When she *(be)* _____

late for an appointment, she *(begin)* _____ to feel nervous.

11. Jane is late for work now. She is stuck in traffic. When she *(get)* _____ to

work, she *(tell)* _____ her co-workers about the heavy traffic.

◇ PRACTICE 18. WHAT + DO. (Chart 11-6)
Directions: Make questions for the given answers using a form of **do**.

1. _____ *What are they doing* _____ now?   They're taking a break.

2. _____ yesterday?   They took a break.

3. _____ tomorrow?   They're going to take a break.

4. _____ tomorrow?   They will take a break.

5. _____ at 11:00 every day?   They take a break.

6. _____   She's meeting with the teacher now.

7. _____   We studied at the library last night.

8. _____   She will quit her job.

9. _____   I'm going to apply for a new job.

10. _____   He is a chef at a five-star restaurant.

◇ **PRACTICE 19. Asking about jobs. (Chart 11-6)**
Directions: Make questions for the given answers using a form of **do.**

electrician   auto mechanic   dental assistant

1. _____*What does he do?*_____   He's an electrician.

2. _____   I'm an auto mechanic.

3. _____   We're college students.

4. _____   They're dental assistants.

5. _____   She's an airline pilot.

6. _____   Thomas and Joanne are engineers.

7. _____   You're a truck driver.

◇ **PRACTICE 20. Chapter review.**
Directions: Choose the correct completions.

1. "Is Ryan going to come with us to the soccer game this afternoon?"
   "I'm not sure. He _____ come."
   A. is going to   B. may   C. maybe   D. will

2. "Are you going to be home for your vacation?"
   "No, I _____ be home. I'm going to stay with my cousins in Toronto."
   A. will   B. might   C. won't   D. don't

3. "When _____ your parents going to be here?"
   "In a few minutes."
   A. will   B. do   C. are   D. is

4. "Do you like all the traveling you do with your job?"
   "Yes. When I'm in a new city, I always _____ new things to see and do."
   A. discover   B. discovered   C. discovers   D. will discover

5. "What _____ Andrew do?"

   "He's a salesperson at a computer store."

   　　　A. is　　　　　　B. did　　　　　　C. will　　　　　　D. does

6. "When are you going to pick up the clothes at the dry cleaners?"

   "In a little while. I'm going to stop there before I _____ the children at school."

   　　　A. pick up　　　B. will pick up　　C. picked up　　D. am going to pick up

7. "Why is the dog barking?"

   "I don't know. _____ someone is outside."

   　　　A. May　　　　　B. Is　　　　　　C. Maybe　　　　　D. Did

8. "What _____ you doing?"

   "We're looking at pictures of our trip."

   　　　A. do　　　　　　B. were　　　　　C. will　　　　　D. are

CHAPTER 12
Modals, Part 1: Expressing Ability

◇ **PRACTICE 1. CAN.** (Chart 12-1)

Directions: Create your own chart by completing each sentence with the correct form of **can + speak**.

1. I   <u>   can speak   </u>   some English.

2. You   _____   some English.

3. He   _____   some English.

4. She   _____   some English.

5. We   _____   some English.

6. They   _____   some English.

7. Tim and I   _____   some English.

8. You and your friend   _____   some English.

9. My teacher   _____   some English.

10. The Yangs   _____   some English.

11. Mrs. Vu   _____   some English.

◇ **PRACTICE 2. CAN/CAN'T.** (Chart 12-1)

Directions: Circle the correct answer in each sentence.

1. Dogs (can,) *can't*   swim.

2. Dogs   *can, can't*   climb trees.

3. Cars   *can, can't*   fly.

4. Machines   *can, can't*   talk.

5. People   *can, can't*   solve problems.

6. Animals   *can, can't*   communicate with other animals.

◇ **PRACTICE 3. CAN/CAN'T.** (Chart 12-1)

Directions: Make sentences about what you and other people *can* and *can't* do. Use words from the list or your own words.

run fast	play the guitar	fly an airplane	repair a computer
read Chinese characters	do algebra	sail a sailboat	speak two languages fluently

1. I _____ .

2. I _____ .

3. I _____ .

4. My best friend _____ .

5. My best friend _____ .

6. My *(a person in your family)* _____ .

7. My *(a person in your family)* _____ .

8. My teacher _____ .

◇ **PRACTICE 4. CAN/CAN'T.** (Charts 12-1 and 12-3)

Directions: Make questions and answers using the given information.

	MIA	GEORGE	PAUL	EVA
drive a car	yes	yes	no	no
play the piano	no	yes	yes	yes
repair a bike	yes	no	yes	no
swim	yes	yes	yes	yes

1. Mia \ drive a car

    Can Mia drive a car? Yes, she can.

2. George and Eva \ play the piano

    _____

3. George \ repair a bike

    _____

4. Paul \ play the piano

    _____

5. Mia, George, Paul \ swim

_____

6. Paul and Eva \ drive a car

_____

Make questions and answers about yourself.

7. you \ play the piano

_____

8. you \ swim

_____

9. you \ repair a bike

_____

◇ PRACTICE 5. CAN/CAN'T. (Charts 12-1 and 12-3)
   Directions: Read the want ad and look at John's skills. Write interview questions and answers using the given information. Use **can** or **can't**.

Job opening at small, international hotel. _Need person with the following: good typing and word-processing skills, excellent knowledge of English, friendly manner on the phone. Also needs to help guests with their suitcases and be available weekends._	John can:

John can:
✔ type
✔ do word processing
_____ speak English
_____ lift suitcases
✔ work weekends

HOTEL MANAGER'S QUESTIONS

1. _____Can you type?_____

2. _____

3. _____

4. _____

5. _____

JOHN'S ANSWERS

_____Yes, I can._____

_____

_____

_____

_____

◇ PRACTICE 6. KNOW HOW TO. (Chart 12-4)
   Directions: Rewrite the sentences using **know how to**.

1. Toni can make pizza.

      Toni knows how to make pizza.

2. Martha can play chess.

_____

3. Sonya and Thomas can speak Portuguese.

_____

4. Jack can't speak Russian.

_____

5. My brothers can't cook.

_____

6. I can't change a flat tire.

_____

flat tire

7. We can't play musical instruments.

_____

8. Can you type?

_____

9. Can your children swim?

_____

10. Can Ari use a digital camera?

_____

◇ PRACTICE 7. KNOW HOW TO. (Chart 12-4)

Directions: Write sentences about what you and others **know how to** do or **don't know how to** do. Use the words from the list or your own words.

make candy	*do word processing*
sew clothes	*cook rice*
use chopsticks	*milk a cow*
do advanced math	*knit*
drive a stick-shift car	*dance*

stick shift

1. I _____.

2. I _____.

3. *(name of your best friend)* _____ .

4. My best friend and I _____ .

5. *(name of a cousin)* _____ .

6. *(name of a classmate)* _____ .

7. *(name of a classmate)* _____ .

◇ **PRACTICE 8. COULD. (Chart 12-5)**

Directions: Stefan and Heidi decided to live without electricity for one month. Write what they **could** and **couldn't** do for that month.

✓ watch TV	spend time together	use electric heat
cook over a fire	use a computer	have heat from a woodstove
read books	turn on the lights	play board games

1. _____*They couldn't watch TV.*_____

2. _____

3. _____

4. _____

5. _____

6. _____

7. _____

8. _____

9. _____

◇ **PRACTICE 9. CAN/COULD. (Charts 12-1 and 12-5)**
Directions: Choose the correct answer in each sentence.

1. Yesterday we *can't*, (*couldn't*) go to the beach. It rained all day.

2. Please turn down the music! I *can't*, *couldn't* study.

3. *Could*, *Can* you speak English a few years ago?

4. I'm a fast typist. I *can*, *could* type 90 words-per-minute on my computer.

5. Sam *could*, *can* tell time when he was four years old.

6. *Could*, *can* you finish the math test yesterday?

7. Our neighbors *can't*, *couldn't* control their dog. She needs dog-obedience classes.

◇ **PRACTICE 10. CAN/COULD. (Charts 12-1 and 12-5)**
Directions: Two months ago, Arturo fell off his bike and broke his leg. He was in a cast for six weeks. Now he is okay. Write what he ***couldn't*** do two months ago and ***can*** do now. Use the appropriate phrases from the list.

✓ *drive a car*	*watch TV*
talk on the phone	*play soccer*
go swimming	*ride a bike*
do homework	*listen to music*

1. Two months ago, ___*he couldn't drive a car.*___ Now, ___*he can drive a car.*___

2. Two months ago, _____ Now, _____

3. Two months ago, _____ Now, _____

4. Two months ago, _____ Now, _____

◇ PRACTICE 11. CAN/COULD. (Charts 12-1 and 12-5)
Directions: Complete the sentences with *can, can't, could,* or *couldn't*.

1. When I was a newborn baby, I _____couldn't_____ walk.

2. When I was a newborn baby, I _____ talk.

3. When I entered kindergarten, I _____ read and write my language.

4. A few years ago, I _____ speak a lot of English.

5. Now I _____ read and write some English.

6. I _____ understand native English speakers well.

7. I _____ always understand my English teacher.

◇ PRACTICE 12. BE ABLE TO. (Chart 12-6)
Directions: Make sentences with the present, past, and future forms of *be able to*.

	ABLE TO (PRESENT)	ABLE TO (PAST)	ABLE TO (FUTURE)
1. I can run.	I am able to run.	I was able to run.	I will be able to run.
2. You can draw.	_____	_____	_____
3. He can drive.	_____	_____	_____
4. She can swim.	_____	_____	_____
5. We can dance.	_____	_____	_____
6. They can type.	_____	_____	_____

◇ PRACTICE 13. BE ABLE TO. (Chart 12-6)
Directions: Make sentences with the present and past forms of *be able to*.

1. When I was a newborn baby, I _____wasn't able to_____ walk.

2. When I was a newborn baby, I _____ talk.

3. When I entered kindergarten, I _____ read and write my language.

4. A few years ago, I _____ speak a lot of English.

5. Now I _____ read and write some English.

6. I _____ understand native English speakers well now.

7. I _____ understand my English teacher all the time.

◇ **PRACTICE 14. BE ABLE TO.** (Chart 12-6)

Directions: Rewrite the boldfaced verbs with the correct form of *be able to*.

wasn't able to speak

Five years ago, Chang was in Australia. He **couldn't speak** any English. He had a

1

difficult time communicating. He **couldn't ask** questions. People **couldn't give** him

2   3

directions. Many times he got lost. He **couldn't visit** tourist sites he was interested in.

4

He was frustrated because he **couldn't have** conversations with people.

5

So Chang decided to study English. Four years later, he went back to Australia.

He was surprised he **could understand** so much. People **could have** long conversations

6   7

with him. He **could learn** about local customs. He **could visit** interesting tourist areas.

8   9

This time Chang had a great trip. Learning English made a big difference.

◇ **PRACTICE 15. BE ABLE TO.** (Chart 12-6)

Directions: Choose the sentence that is closest in meaning to the given sentence.

1. James can run very fast.
   a. He will be able to run very fast.
   b. He is able to run very fast.
   c. He was able to run very fast.

2. I will be able to have dinner with you.
   a. I can have dinner with you.
   b. I could have dinner with you.
   c. I was able to have dinner with you.

3. Jean couldn't finish her science project.
   a. She isn't able to finish her science project.
   b. She wasn't able to finish her science project.
   c. She won't be able to finish her science project.

4. My roommate wasn't able to come to the party.
   a. He won't be able to come to the party.
   b. He can't come to the party.
   c. He couldn't come to the party.

5. I can't help you later.
    a. I wasn't able to help you.
    b. I couldn't help you.
    c. I won't be able to help you.

◇ PRACTICE 16. VERY/TOO. (Chart 12-7)
    Directions: Complete the sentences with *very* or *too*.

1. This leather coat is _____ too _____ expensive. I can't buy it.

2. The tea is _____ hot, but I can drink it.

3. The clothing store is _____ big. There's a good selection.

4. The neighbors are _____ noisy. I want them to move.

5. The Arctic Circle is _____ cold. I don't want to travel there.

6. These pants are _____ short. I'm not going to buy them.

7. My teacher talks _____ fast. It's good practice for me.

8. This car is _____ small. It won't use a lot of gas.

◇ PRACTICE 17. VERY/TOO. (Chart 12-7)
    Directions: Choose the best completion for each sentence.

1. Do you like this book?
    A. Yes, it's very interesting.   B. Yes, it's too interesting.

2. I can't watch this movie.
    A. It's too violent.   B. It's very violent.

3. You had no mistakes on your math test.
    A. Your knowledge of math is too good.   B. Your knowledge of math is very good.

4. We can do these math problems.
    A. They're too easy.   B. They're very easy.

5. This dress is too tight.
    A. I can't wear it.   B. I can wear it.

6. This puzzle looks very tricky.
    A. Let's see if we can figure it out.   B. It will be impossible to do.

7. Thomas is too friendly.
    A. I feel comfortable around him.   B. I feel uncomfortable around him.

8. Let's buy this mattress.
    A. It's very comfortable.   B. It's too comfortable.

◇ PRACTICE 18. VERY/TOO. (Chart 12-7)
Directions: Write answers to the questions.

1. What school subjects are very hard for you?

_____

2. What school subjects are too hard for you?

_____

3. What foods do you think are very spicy?

_____

4. What foods are too spicy for you?

_____

5. What cities have climates that are too hot for you?

_____

6. What cities have climates that are too cold for you?

_____

◇ PRACTICE 19. TWO/TOO/TO. (Chart 12-8)
Directions: Complete the sentences with *two, too,* or *to.*

1. I have _____ *two* _____ children.

2. Let's go _____ the mall.

3. I can't hear the phone ring. The TV is _____ loud. The radio is loud _____.

4. I spoke with Alex. Did you talk _____ Alex _____?

5. Where do you want _____ go? _____ the beach? _____ the park?

6. Jenny is 10 years old. She is _____ young for makeup. Her friends are

_____.

7. _____ dogs followed me _____ school today.

8. Some dogs followed me _____.

◇ PRACTICE 20. TWO/TOO/TO. (Chart 12-8)
Directions: Complete the sentences with *two, too,* or *to.*

My husband and I have _____ *two* _____ daughters.
                              1

They are quite different. My older daughter is very friendly.

She likes _____ meet people and make new friends. She loves _____ talk
                2   3

on the phone with her friends. Some parents think she is _____ talkative.
                                                                          4

My younger daughter is shy. She likes _____ spend time reading or playing
                                                   5

with her pets. She has a small zoo at our house. She has _____ cats, some rabbits,
                                                                         6

a bird, _____ fish, and even a horse.
              7

Fortunately, my daughters enjoy each other. They love _____ spend time with
                                                                       8

each other, and they're best friends _____ .
                                              9

◇ PRACTICE 21. AT/IN. (Chart 12-9)
Directions: Complete the sentences with **at** or **in**.

Last week, Ben was . . .

1. _____*at*_____ home.

2. _____ school for a meeting.

3. _____ work.

4. _____ the bedroom.

5. _____ bed.

6. _____ the hospital visiting a friend.

7. _____ the post office.

8. _____ class.

9. _____ his hometown of Mountain View.

10. on the phone with someone _____ jail.

◇ PRACTICE 22. AT/IN. (Chart 12-9)
Directions: Complete the sentences about the Johnson family. Use **in** or **at**.

It's 10:00 A.M. Where is everyone?

1. Mr. Johnson is _____*in*_____ his office _____*at*_____ work.

2. Mrs. Johnson is _____ the library with her first grade class.

3. Joe is _____ class _____ school.

4. Beth is sick _____ home _____ bed.

5. Rita is on vacation _____ Hawaii.

6. Bob is _____ work. He is working _____ a bookstore.

7. Grandma Johnson is _____ the hospital. She is very sick.

◇ **PRACTICE 23. Chapter review.**

Directions: Choose the correct completions.

1. _____ play a musical instrument?
   A. Do you can   B. Can you   C. Do you be able to   D. Can you to

2. I _____ my homework. I was too tired.
   A. couldn't to finish   B. could finish   C. couldn't finish   D. couldn't finished

3. I don't know how _____ to the Palace Hotel from here.
   A. do I get   B. get   C. getting   D. to get

4. Gina _____ understand the speaker at the lecture last night.
   A. couldn't   B. doesn't able to   C. won't be able to   D. can't

5. My uncle can't _____ English.
   A. to speak   B. speaking   C. speaks   D. speak

6. Rosa works for a computer company _____ Taipei.
   A. on   B. at   C. in   D. to

7. The library has a _____ comfortable reading room. I spend a lot of time there.
   A. too   B. two   C. very   D. to

8. The thief is _____ prison for five years.
   A. at   B. in   C. to   D. on

◇ **PRACTICE 24. Verb review.**

Directions: Complete the sentences. Use the words in parentheses. Use any appropriate verb form.

Once upon a time there (be) _____ *was* _____ *a mouse named Young Mouse. He*
                                      1

lived near a river with his family and friends. Every day he and the other mice did the same things.

They (hunt) _____ *hunted* _____ *for food and* (take) _____ *care of their*
                      2   3

mouse holes. In the evening they (listen) _____ *to stories around a fire.*
                                              4

Young Mouse especially liked to listen to stories about the Far Away Land. He (dream)

_____ *about the Far Away Land. It sounded wonderful. One day he* (decide)
        5

_____ *to go there.*
        6

YOUNG MOUSE: Goodbye, Old Mouse. I'm leaving now.

OLD MOUSE: Why *(you, leave)*

_____7_____? Where

(you, go) _____8_____?

YOUNG MOUSE: I *(go)* _____9_____ to a new and different place. I *(go)*

_____10_____ to the Far Away Land.

OLD MOUSE: Why *(you, want)* _____11_____ *(go)* _____12_____ there?

YOUNG MOUSE: I *(want)* _____13_____ *(experience)* _____14_____

all of life. I *(need)* _____15_____ *(learn)* _____16_____ about everything.

OLD MOUSE: You *(can learn)* _____17_____ many things if you *(stay)*

_____18_____ here with us. Please *(stay)* _____19_____ here with us.

YOUNG MOUSE: No, I *(can stay, not)* _____20_____ here by the river for the rest

of my life. There *(be)* _____21_____ too much to learn about in the world. I must go to the Far Away Land.

OLD MOUSE: The trip to the Far Away Land is a long and dangerous journey. You *(have)*

_____22_____ many problems before you *(get)* _____23_____

there. You *(face)* _____24_____ many dangers.

YOUNG MOUSE: I understand that, but I need to find out about the Far Away Land.

Goodbye, Old Mouse. Goodbye, everyone! I *(may see, never)* _____25_____

any of you again, but I *(try)* _____26_____ to return from the Far Away Land someday. Goodbye!

So Young Mouse left to fulfill his dream of going to the Far Away Land. His first problem was the river. At the river, he met a frog.

MAGIC FROG: Hello, Young Mouse. I'm Magic Frog. *(you, have)* _____27_____

a problem right now?

YOUNG MOUSE: Yes. How *(I, can cross)* _____28_____ this river? I *(know, not)*

_____29_____ how to swim. If I *(can cross, not)* _____30_____ this

river, I *(be, not)* _____31_____ able to reach the Far Away Land.

Modals, Part 1: Expressing Ability **195**

MAGIC FROG: I (help) _____ you to cross the river. I (give)
                            32

_____ you the power of my legs so you (can jump)
        33

_____ across the river. I (give, also) _____
        34   35

you a new name. Your new name will be Jumping Mouse.

JUMPING MOUSE: Thank you, Magic Frog.

MAGIC FROG: You are a brave mouse, Jumping Mouse,

and you have a good heart. If you (lose, not)

_____ hope, you (reach)
        36

_____ the Far Away Land.
        37

*With his powerful new legs, Jumping Mouse jumped
across the river. He traveled fast for many days across a wide
grassland. One day he met a buffalo. The buffalo was lying on the ground.*

JUMPING MOUSE: Hello, Buffalo. My name is Jumping Mouse. Why (you, lie★)

_____ on the ground? (you, be) _____ ill?
        38   39

BUFFALO: Yes. I (can see, not) _____ . I (drink) _____
                                        40   41

some poisoned water, and now I (be) _____ blind. I (die)
                                                42

_____ soon because I (can find, not) _____ food
        43   44

and water without my eyes.

JUMPING MOUSE: When I started my journey, Magic Frog (give) _____
                                                                            45

me her powerful legs so I could jump across the river. What (I, can give)

_____ you to help you? I know! I (give) _____
        46   47

you my sight so you can see to find food and water.

BUFFALO: Are you really going to do that? Jumping Mouse, you are very kind! Ah! Yes, I

(can see) _____ again. Thank you! But now you (can see, not)
                    48

_____ . How (you, find) _____ the Far Away
        49   50

★The *-ing* form of *lie* is spelled *lying*.

Land? I know. *(jump)* _____ onto my back. I *(carry)*
_____ you across this land to the foot of the mountain.
JUMPING MOUSE: Thank you, Buffalo.

So Jumping Mouse found a way to reach the mountain. When they reached the mountain,
Jumping Mouse and Buffalo parted.

BUFFALO: I don't live in the mountains, so I *(can go, not)* _____ any
farther.
JUMPING MOUSE: What *(I, do)* _____ ? I *(have)* _____
powerful legs, but I can't see.
BUFFALO: *(keep)* _____ your hope alive. You *(find)* _____
a way to reach the Far Away Land.

Jumping Mouse was very afraid. He didn't know what to do. Suddenly he heard a wolf.

JUMPING MOUSE: Hello? Wolf? I *(can see, not)* _____ you, but I
(can hear) _____ you.
WOLF: Yes, Jumping Mouse. I'm here, but I *(can help, not)* _____ you
because I *(die★)* _____.
JUMPING MOUSE: What's wrong? Why *(you, die)* _____ ?
WOLF: I *(lose)* _____ my sense of smell many weeks ago, so now I
(can find, not) _____ food. I *(starve)* _____ to death.
JUMPING MOUSE: Oh, Wolf, I *(can help)* _____ you. I *(give)*
_____ you my ability to smell.
WOLF: Oh, thank you, Jumping Mouse. Yes, I *(can smell)* _____ again.
Now I'll be able to find food. That is a wonderful gift! How *(I, can help)*
_____ you?
JUMPING MOUSE: I *(try)* _____ to get to the Far Away Land. I *(need)*
_____ *(go)* _____ to the top of the mountain.
WOLF: *(come)* _____ over here. I *(put)* _____ you on
my back and *(take)* _____ you to the top of the mountain.

_____
★The *-ing* form of *die* is spelled *dying.*

So Wolf carried Jumping Mouse to the top of the mountain. But then Wolf left. Jumping Mouse was all alone. He (can see, not) _____ and he (can smell, not)
76
_____, *but he still had powerful legs.* He almost (lose) _____
77   78
hope. *Then suddenly, he* (hear) _____ *Magic Frog.*
79

JUMPING MOUSE: Is that you, Magic Frog? Please *(help)* _____ me. I'm
80
all alone and afraid.

MAGIC FROG: *(cry, not)* _____ , Jumping Mouse. You have a generous,
81
open heart. You *(be, not)* _____ selfish. You help others. Your
82
unselfishness caused you suffering during your journey, but you *(lose, never)*

_____ hope. Now you are in the Far Away Land. *(jump)*
83

_____ , Jumping Mouse. *(use)* _____ your
84   85
powerful legs to jump high in the air. Jump! Jump!

Jumping Mouse jumped as high as he could, up, up, up. He reached his arms out to his sides and started to fly. He felt strong and powerful.

JUMPING MOUSE: I can fly! I can fly! I *(fly)* _____!
86
MAGIC FROG: Jumping Mouse, I am going to give you a new name. Now your name is Eagle!

*So Jumping Mouse became the powerful Eagle and fulfilled his dream of reaching the Far Away Land and experiencing all that life has to offer.**

---

*This fable is based on a Native American story and has been adapted from *The Story of Jumping Mouse* by John Steptoe; Lothrop, Lee & Shepard books, 1984.

CHAPTER 13

Modals, Part 2: Advice, Necessity, Requests, Suggestions

◇ **PRACTICE 1. SHOULD.** (Chart 13-1)

Directions: Create your own chart by completing each sentence with the correct form of **should + study.**

1. Mrs. Wang _____*should study*_____ more.

2. He _____ more.

3. We _____ more.

4. You _____ more.

5. She _____ more.

6. They _____ more.

7. Nick _____ more.

8. I _____ more.

9. The students _____ more.

◇ **PRACTICE 2. SHOULD.** (Chart 13-1)

Directions: Complete the sentences with **should** or **shouldn't.**

Sami wants to be on his high school soccer team.

1. He _____*should*_____ practice kicking a ball with his friends.

2. He _____ exercise a lot.

3. He _____ smoke cigarettes.

4. He _____ stop doing homework so he has more time for soccer.

5. He _____ practice running fast.

6. He _____ watch famous soccer games.

7. He _____ eat a lot of snack foods.

◇ **PRACTICE 3. SHOULD. (Chart 13-1)**

Directions: Write sentences with **should** or **shouldn't**.

Rose gets failing grades in school. She wants to get better grades.

1. She doesn't do her homework.

    She should do her homework.

2. She copies her roommate's homework.

    She shouldn't copy her roommate's homework.

3. She doesn't study for her tests.

    _____

4. She stays up late.

    _____

5. She daydreams in class.

    _____

6. She is absent from class a lot.

    _____

7. She doesn't take notes during lectures.

    _____

8. She doesn't take her books to school.

    _____

◇ **PRACTICE 4. SHOULD. (Chart 13-1)**

Directions: Give advice. Use **should** or **shouldn't**.

1. Sara's bedroom is very messy. She can't find her clothes.

    Sara _____*should clean her room.*_____

2. The Browns play loud music at night. It wakes up the neighbors.

    The neighbors _____

3. Janet is a dance teacher. She has a backache.

    Janet _____

4. Bill has a sore tooth. It began to hurt four weeks ago.

    Bill _____

5. Ronnie isn't careful with his money. He spends too much and he's always broke.*

Ronnie _____

6. Mr. and Mrs. Brown are traveling to South America soon. They don't have visas.

They _____

◇ PRACTICE 5. HAVE TO/HAS TO. (Chart 13-2)
Directions: Create your own chart by completing each sentence with the correct form of **have to/has to** + **leave**.

1. I _____*have to leave*_____ soon.

2. We _____ soon.

3. They _____ soon.

4. You _____ soon.

5. He _____ soon.

6. She _____ soon.

7. My parents (not) _____ soon.

8. The children (not) _____ soon.

9. Mark (not) _____ soon.

10. Mark and I (not) _____ soon.

◇ PRACTICE 6. HAVE TO/HAS TO. (Chart 13-2)
Directions: Complete the sentences with **has to** or **doesn't have to**.

Roger wants to be a children's doctor. What qualities does he have to have?

1. He _____*has to*_____ be smart.

2. He ____*doesn't have to*____ be good-looking.

3. He _____ be patient.

4. He _____ speak several languages.

5. He _____ be athletic.

6. He _____ like children.

7. He _____ like working with sick people.

_____

*broke = have no money.

◇ **PRACTICE 7. HAVE TO/HAS TO. (Chart 13-2)**
Directions: Complete each sentence with *have to/has to* or *don't have to/doesn't have to*.

1. We _____*have to*_____ leave now. Our class starts soon.

2. We _____ hurry. We're almost there.

3. A good teacher _____ begin on time.

4. The students _____ arrive on time. Late students get lower grades.

5. Students _____ arrive before 8:00. The school isn't open.

6. I _____ study hard. I want to go to medical school.

7. Jane _____ take difficult science classes. She wants to be an artist.

8. Teachers _____ correct a lot of homework. They collect it every day.

9. My teacher _____ correct a lot of papers. She has 50 students.

10. My friend's teacher has five students. She _____ correct a lot of papers.

◇ **PRACTICE 8. HAD TO/DIDN'T HAVE TO. (Chart 13-2)**
Directions: Complete each sentence with *had to* or *didn't have to*.

Mr. Napoli is retired now. For thirty years, he owned a successful bakery. His bakery opened at 5:00 A.M. and closed at 7:00 P.M. What did he have to or didn't have to do?

1. He _____*had to*_____ work hard.

2. He _____ get up early.

3. His home was above the bakery. He _____ take the bus to work.

4. He _____ be friendly to his customers.

5. His wife took the children to school. He _____ take them.

6. He _____ work long hours.

7. His workers did the cleaning. He _____ clean up at night.

8. He _____ begin baking before 5:00 A.M.

◇ PRACTICE 9. HAD TO/DIDN'T HAVE TO. (Chart 13-2)
   Directions: Complete each sentence with **had to** or **didn't have to**.

What did you have to do when you were a child?

1. I ___*had to / didn't have to*___ keep my bedroom clean.

2. I _____ cook dinner for my family.

3. I _____ make my lunch for school.

4. I _____ help my parents.

5. I _____ wash my own clothes.

6. I _____ be nice to my siblings (brothers and sisters).

7. I _____ feed the pets.

8. I _____ be polite to my parents.

◇ PRACTICE 10. SHOULD, HAVE TO, and DON'T HAVE TO. (Charts 13-1 and 13-2)
   Directions: Complete each sentence with **should**, **have to**, or **don't have to**.

High school students in my country . . .

1. ___*should / have to / don't have to*___ work hard.

2. _____ go to school on Saturdays.

3. _____ stand up when the teacher comes in the room.

4. _____ clean the classroom after class.

5. _____ do homework every day.

6. _____ take extra classes after school or in the evening.

7. _____ memorize a lot of information.

8. _____ work together in small groups.

9. _____ be polite to other students.

10. _____ bring a dictionary to class.

11. _____ go to school on Saturdays.

12. _____ wear uniforms to school.

◇ PRACTICE 11. MUST/MUST NOT. (Chart 13-3)
Directions: Complete each sentence with ***must*** or ***must not***.

SWIMMING POOL RULES

1. Swimmers _____*must*_____ take a shower before entering the pool.

2. Small children _____ be with a parent.

3. Non-swimmers _____ go in the deep end of the pool.

4. Non-swimmers _____ wear lifejackets.

5. Swimmers _____ dive in the shallow* end of the pool.

6. Non-swimmers _____ jump off the diving board.

◇ PRACTICE 12. MUST/MUST NOT. (Chart 13-3)
Directions: Complete each sentence with ***must*** or ***must not***.

Beth is going to have serious surgery. What is her doctor going to tell
her after the surgery?

1. She _____*must*_____ take her medicine.

2. She _____ go to work the next day.

—————————
**shallow* = opposite of *deep*.

3. She _____ rest.

4. She _____ lift heavy objects for several weeks.

5. She _____ call her doctor if she gets a fever.

6. She _____ stay quiet.

◇ PRACTICE 13. MUST/SHOULD. (Charts 13-1 and 13-3)
   Directions: Complete each sentence with **must** or **should**.

1. You ____*should*____ make your bed every day. Your bedroom looks nicer when you

   make it.

2. You _____*must*_____ wear a seat belt on an airplane when the seat belt sign is on.

3. You _____ have I.D. to get on an airplane. People without I.D. cannot get

   on the plane.

4. You _____ take vitamins every day. They may help you stay healthy.

5. You _____ obey the speed limit. If you drive too fast, you will get a ticket.

6. You _____ bring your dictionary to writing class, but if you don't, you can

   use the teacher's.

7. If you want to go to a top university, you _____ have good grades.

8. You _____ watch movies if you want to improve your English.

9. You _____ rest when you are tired.

◇ **PRACTICE 14. MAY I, COULD I, CAN I.** (Chart 13-4)
  Directions: Make polite questions using *May I, Could I,* or *Can I.*

  1. You are at a restaurant. Your coffee is cold. You want hot coffee.

      May I / Could I / Can I have some hot coffee please?

  2. You are in class. You want to look at your classmate's dictionary for a minute.

      _____

  3. You are taking a test. You want to sharpen your pencil.

      _____

  4. You are stuck in traffic with your friend. You want to borrow her cell phone.

      _____

  5. You are in the library. You lost your library card. You need a new one.

      _____

◇ **PRACTICE 15. COULD YOU/WOULD YOU.** (Chart 13-5)
  Directions: Write polite questions with *Could you* or *Would you.*

  1. You didn't hear your teacher's question. You want him/her to repeat it.

      Could / Would you please repeat the question?

  2. You are a parent. You want your teenager to clean his bedroom.

      _____

  3. You are a teenager. You want your parent to give you some money for a movie.

      _____

  4. You are at home. You want your roommate to turn down the TV.

      _____

  5. You are at a restaurant. The server brings you cream for your coffee and it is sour. You want some fresh cream.

      _____

  6. You are at a park with your friends. You want someone to take a picture of all of you. You ask a person nearby.

      _____

◇ **PRACTICE 16. Imperative sentences.** (Chart 13-6)
  Directions: <u>Underline</u> the imperative verbs in the following conversations.

  1. MICHELLE: May I come in?
      PROFESSOR: Certainly. <u>Come</u> in. How can I help you?

MICHELLE: I need to ask you a question about yesterday's lecture.
PROFESSOR: Okay. What's the question?

2. STUDENT: Do we have any homework for tomorrow?
   TEACHER: Yes. Read pages 24 through 36, and answer the questions on page 37, in writing.
   STUDENT: Is that all?
   TEACHER: Yes.

3. HEIDI: Please close the window, Mike. It's a little chilly in here.
   MIKE: Okay. Is there anything else I can do for you before I leave?
   HEIDI: Could you turn off the light in the kitchen?
   MIKE: No problem. Anything else?
   HEIDI: Ummm, please hand me the remote control for the TV. It's over there.
   MIKE: Sure. Here.
   HEIDI: Thanks.
   MIKE: I'll stop by again tomorrow. Take care of yourself. Take good care of that broken leg.
   HEIDI: Don't worry. I will. Thanks again.

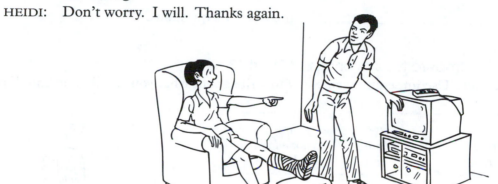

◇ **PRACTICE 17. Imperative sentences. (Chart 13-6)**
Directions: Describe how to make popcorn. Put the sentences in the correct order.

MAKING POPCORN THE OLD-FASHIONED WAY

_____ Stop shaking the pan when the popcorn stops popping.

_____ Put the popcorn in a pan.

_____ Shake the pan.

_____ Pour the popcorn into a bowl.

_____ Cover the pan with a lid.

_____ Pour melted butter over the popcorn.

_____ Heat the oil.

___1___ Put some oil in a pan.

_____ Salt the popcorn.

_____ Enjoy your snack!

◇ **PRACTICE 18. Imperative sentences. (Chart 13-6)**

Directions: Use imperative sentences to write what you should and shouldn't do at school.

✓sit	copy	do	work	answer	✓chew	talk

SCHOOL RULES

1. _____Sit_____ quietly in class.

2. ___Don't chew___ gum in class.

3. _____ to your friends when the teacher is talking.

4. _____ your homework.

5. _____ your classmates' homework.

6. _____ hard.

7. _____ the teacher's questions.

◇ **PRACTICE 19. Imperative sentences. (Chart 13-6)**

Directions: Use imperative sentences to write about what you should and shouldn't do.

ask	use	follow
turn off	✓bring	download
✓show	play	talk

COMPUTER LAB RULES AT SCHOOL

1. _____Show_____ your I.D. to the lab director when you enter the lab.

2. ___Don't bring___ food or drinks into the computer lab.

3. _____ the lab director's instructions.

4. _____ your cell phone.

5. _____ computer games.

6. _____ the computers for school work.

7. _____ in a quiet voice.

8. _____ the lab assistant for help if you are having trouble.

9. _____ music from the Internet.

◇ PRACTICE 20. Modal auxiliaries. (Chart 13-7)
   Directions: Add **to** where necessary. If **to** is not necessary, write **Ø**.

1. The sky is dark. It is going _____*to*_____ rain.

2. Would you please _____ speak more slowly?

3. You should _____ meet John. He's very interesting.

4. Do we have _____ have a test tomorrow?

5. Will you _____ join us for lunch?

6. Robert might not _____ work tomorrow. He doesn't feel well.

7. I'm not able _____ help you right now.

8. The neighbors shouldn't _____ have loud parties late at night.

9. We weren't able _____ use our e-mail yesterday.

10. Monica can't _____ talk much because she has a bad cough.

◇ PRACTICE 21. Modal review. (Chart 13-8)
   Directions: Choose the sentence that is closest in meaning.

1. We must leave.
   a. We should leave.
   b. We have to leave.
   c. We may leave.

2. I wasn't able to come.
   a. I couldn't come.
   b. I didn't have to come.
   c. I shouldn't come.

3. Mrs. Jones will pick us up tomorrow.
   a. Mrs. Jones may pick us up.
   b. Mrs. Jones is going to pick us up.
   c. Mrs. Jones could pick us up.

4. I'm not able to meet with you tomorrow.
   a. I won't meet with you.
   b. I don't have to meet with you.
   c. I can't meet with you.

5. Would you close the door please?
   a. Should you close the door?
   b. Must you close the door?
   c. Could you close the door?

6. You should take a break.
   a. You have to take a break.
   b. You might take a break.
   c. It's a good idea for you to take a break.

7. Tom didn't have to work yesterday.
   a. Tom didn't need to work yesterday.
   b. Tom couldn't work yesterday.
   c. Tom didn't want to work yesterday.

8. It might be stormy tomorrow.
   a. It must be stormy tomorrow.
   b. It may be stormy tomorrow.
   c. It will be stormy tomorrow.

◇ PRACTICE 22. LET'S. (Chart 13-9)
   Directions: Write a response with **Let's**.

   1. A: The sun is shining. It's going to be a warm day.

      B: ___*Let's go to the park.*_____

   2. A: We worked hard today.

      B: _____

   3. A: Sandra's birthday is this weekend.

      B: _____

   4. A: Breakfast is ready.

      B: _____

   5. A: Mario's Pizzeria is having a special tonight: free pizza for kids.

      B: _____

◇ PRACTICE 23. Chapter review.
   Directions: Choose the correct completion for each sentence.

   1. It's very late and I have to get up early. I _____ go to bed.
      A. can   B. should   C. had to

   2. We _____ up late last night. We had a lot of homework.
      A. have to stay   B. had to stayed   C. had to stay

3. It's a beautiful day. Let's _____ to the beach.
    A. going   B. to go   C. go

4. Please be quiet. I _____ the speaker very well.
    A. can't hear   B. am not hearing   C. couldn't hear

5. It's hot in here. _____ the window please?
    A. You will open   B. Could you open   C. Should you open

6. Excuse me. _____ me lift this box?
    A. Would you help   B. Would you to help   C. Would you helping

7. _____ leave now? We're having so much fun.
    A. Do we has to   B. Are we have to   C. Do we have to

8. Mia _____ pay for her groceries. She lost her wallet in the store.
    A. wasn't able   B. couldn't   C. can't to

9. We're excited. It _____ snow tonight or tomorrow.
    A. can   B. must   C. might

10. You _____ take this medicine. You are very, very sick.
    A. must   B. could   C. might

◇ PRACTICE 1. Nouns and adjectives. (Chart 14-1)

Directions: How are the words in the list usually used? Write them in the correct column.

✓ *tall*	*pens*	*boat*	*true*
pretty	*sad*	*store*	*happy*
✓ *clothes*	*hot*	*horse*	*truth*

ADJECTIVES	NOUNS
tall	clothes

◇ PRACTICE 2. Nouns and adjectives. (Chart 14-1)

Directions: Make adjective + noun phrases. Use the words in the list. You may use a word more than once.

soup	*sad*	*nutritious*	*language*	*interesting*	*boring*
grammar	*chicken*	*funny*	*English*	*song*	*book*
happy	*person*	*story*	*wonderful*	*news*	*food*

1. _interesting (happy / sad / funny / boring / wonderful) song_

2. _____

3. _____

4. _____

5. _____

6. _____

7. _____

8. _____

9. _____

10. _____

◇ PRACTICE 3. Nouns and adjectives. (Chart 14-1)
Directions: How is the underlined word used? Circle **adjective** or **noun**.

1. The <u>camera</u> store has photography classes. (adjective) noun

2. Do you have a digital <u>camera</u>? adjective noun

3. What are you going to order for <u>lunch</u>? adjective noun

4. Nancy's Cafe has a delicious <u>lunch</u> menu. adjective noun

5. I read an interesting <u>newspaper</u> article today about electric cars. adjective noun

HUMMMMM

6. Do you read the <u>newspaper</u> every day? adjective noun

7. We need to get some dog <u>food</u>. adjective noun

8. The <u>pet</u> store is having a sale. adjective noun

Pet Store

◇ PRACTICE 4. Nouns and adjectives. (Chart 14-1)
Directions: Make two phrases for each given noun: ADJECTIVE + NOUN and NOUN + NOUN.

	ADJECTIVE + NOUN	NOUN + NOUN
1. *traffic*	*heavy traffic*	*traffic sign*
2. *grammar*	_____	_____
3. *apartment*	_____	_____
4. *newspaper*	_____	_____
5. *music*	_____	_____

◇ **PRACTICE 5. Nouns and adjectives. (Chart 14-1)**

Directions: Complete the sentences. Use the information in the first part of the sentence. Use a noun that modifies another noun in the completion.

1. A house for a dog is called a _____ *dog house.* _____

2. An article in a magazine is called a _____

3. A card for business is called a _____

4. An appointment with a dentist is called a _____

5. Salad that has chicken in it is called _____

6. A key for a house is called a _____

7. A printer that is used with a computer is called a _____

8. A carton for milk is called a _____

9. A store that has clothes in it is called a _____

10. A curtain for a shower is called a

_____

shower curtain

◇ **PRACTICE 6. Nouns and adjectives. (Chart 14-1)**

Directions: Use the given words to make common ADJECTIVE + NOUN or NOUN + NOUN PHRASES.

1. **birthday**

   a. *present* _____ *birthday present* _____

   b. *happy* _____ *happy birthday* _____

   c. *cake* _____ *birthday cake* _____

2. **kitchen**

   a. *messy* _____

   b. *cabinets* _____

   c. *counter* _____

3. **bus**

   a. *city* _____

   b. *schedule* _____

   c. *route* _____

4. **airplane**

a. *noise* _____

b. *movie* _____

c. *ticket* _____

5. **apartment**

a. *manager* _____

b. *one-bedroom* _____

c. *building* _____

6. **phone**

a. *number* _____

b. *cell* _____

c. *call* _____

7. **patient**

a. *hospital* _____

b. *sick* _____

c. *information* _____

◇ PRACTICE 7. Word order of adjectives. (Chart 14-2)
   Directions: Write the *italicized* words in the correct order.

1. *house*
   100-year-old
   small

   a ___*small 100-year-old house*_____

2. *spicy*
   food
   Mexican

   some _____

3. *man*
   young
   kind

   a _____

4. *dirty*
   glass
   brown

   a _____

5. *tall*
   lovely
   rose bush

   a _____

6. *small*
   paintings
   interesting
   old

   some _____

7. *film*   an _____
   foreign
   new
   important

8. *yellow*   some _____
   flowers
   little

9. *middle-aged*   a _____
   woman
   tall

10. *cabinet*   an _____
   wooden
   Chinese
   antique

◇ **PRACTICE 8. Word order of adjectives. (Chart 14-2)**
   Directions: Choose the correct completions.

1. We work in _____ office building.
   Ⓐ a large old   B. an old large

2. I spoke with a _____ man at the park today.
   A. Greek friendly   B. friendly Greek

3. I need some _____ socks.
   A. brown comfortable   B. comfortable brown

4. My sister makes _____ soup.
   A. vegetarian delicious   B. delicious vegetarian

5. The children found _____ box at the beach.
   A. an old metal   B. a metal old

6. My family loves _____ food.
   A. spicy Indian   B. Indian spicy

7. Robert gave his girlfriend _____ ring.
   A. an antique beautiful   B. a beautiful antique

8. There is a _____ soccer field near our house.
   A. wonderful big grassy★
   B. grassy big wonderful

_____
★*grassy* = covered with grass.

◇ PRACTICE 9. ALL OF, MOST OF, SOME OF, ALMOST ALL OF. (Chart 14-3)
   Directions: Match the picture with the sentence.

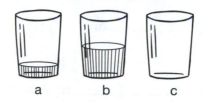

   a   b   c

   1. Meg drank most of the milk. Now the glass looks like _____*a*_____ .

   2. Meg drank all of the milk. Now the glass looks like _____ .

   3. Meg drank some of the milk. Now the glass looks like _____ or _____ .

   4. Meg drank almost all of the milk. Now the glass looks like _____ .

◇ PRACTICE 10. Understanding quantity expressions. (Charts 14-3 and 14-4)
   Directions: Choose the percentage that is closest in meaning to the quantity expression.

   1. Almost all of the students are coming to the picnic.   (95%)   75%   100%

   2. Most of the staff is coming to the picnic.   90%   100%   50%

   3. All of the food for the picnic is ready.   90%   100%   95%

   4. Some of the dishes are very spicy.   100%   60%   0%

   5. Half of the class is bringing a friend.   50%   60%   40%

   6. A lot of people in my class ride bikes to school.   75%   40%   25%

   7. Some of the people in my class have motorcycles.   0%   99%   30%

   8. Most of the teachers take the bus to school.   88%   65%   70%

   9. All of the bus drivers are careful.   97%   90%   100%

   10. Almost all of the drivers are friendly.   97%   100%   80%

◇ PRACTICE 11. Agreement with quantity words. (Chart 14-4)
   Directions: Complete the sentences with *is* or *are*.

   1. All of the work _____*is*_____ correct.

   2. All of the answers _____ correct.

   3. All of the information _____ correct.

   4. All of the facts _____ correct.

   5. Some of your homework _____ incorrect.

6. Some of the students _____ ready.

7. Almost all of the children _____ tired.

8. A lot of the class _____ tired.

9. A lot of the students _____ tired.

10. Half of the vocabulary _____ new for me.

11. Half of the words _____ new for me.

12. Most of the food _____ gone.

13. Some of the food _____ cold.

14. All of the apples _____ from our apple tree.

15. Almost all of the fruit _____ organic.

16. Most of the vegetables _____ fresh.

◇ PRACTICE 12. ONE OF/NONE OF + noun agreement. (Chart 14-5)
Directions: Choose the correct form of the noun in each sentence.

1. One of my *friend,* (*friends*) is Mrs. Rodriguez.

2. One of our *class, classes* has 30 students.

3. My neighbor Mrs. Gold is one of my *teacher, teachers.*

4. One of my favorite *meal, meals* is rice and chicken.

5. One of your *shoe, shoes* is untied.

6. None of my *friend, friends* speak fluent English.

7. None of the new *word, words* is easy for me.

8. None of the *child, children* is absent today.

9. None of the *movie, movies* at the theater look very interesting.

10. Global warming is one of the most serious *problem, problems* we have.

◇ PRACTICE 13. ONE OF/NONE OF + verb agreement. (Chart 14-5)
Directions: Choose the correct verb in each sentence. In some cases, both are correct.

1. None of the stores (*is,*) (*are*) open late.

2. One of the stores (*is,*) *are* closed on weekends.

3. None of the boots *fits, fit* me.

4. One of the coats *fits, fit.*

5. None of the parks in this town *has, have* a swimming pool.

6. One of the parks *has, have* nice tennis courts.

7. None of the teachers at my school *is, are* a native-English speaker.

8. One of my teachers *teaches, teach* judo after school.

9. None of my friends *takes, take* the class.

10. One of my friends *is, are* a karate expert.

11. None of the homework for the weekend *looks, look* very hard.

12. None of the new vocabulary *seems, seem* difficult.

◇ PRACTICE 14. ONE OF/NONE OF. (Chart 14-5)
Directions: Make sentences from the given words and phrases.

1. One of the \ test question \ have \ a mistake

      One of the test questions has a mistake.

2. None of the \ question \ be \ easy

_____

3. One of my \ cousin \ work \ with me

_____

4. None of the \ jewelry \ be \ very valuable

_____

5. None of the \ ring \ be \ very expensive

_____

6. One of my \ teacher \ have \ several grandchildren

_____

◇ **PRACTICE 15. Review: expressions of quantity.** (Charts 14-3 → 14-5)
  Directions: Complete the sentences with the following expressions: ***all of, almost all of, some of, one of,*** or ***none of.***

1. _____One of_____ the men looks serious.

2. _____ the people are children.

3. _____ the people are smiling.

4. _____ the women are unhappy.

5. _____ the people have hats.

6. _____ the men has a mustache.

7. _____ the women have mustaches.

8. _____ the people look old.

9. _____ the people look very young.

10. _____ the people look friendly.

◇ **PRACTICE 16. Review: expressions of quantity.** (Charts 14-3 → 14-5)
  Directions: Choose the correct verb in each sentence.

  1. All of your English work *(is,)* *are* correct.

  2. All of your sentences *is, are* correct.

  3. Some of your math work *is, are* correct.

  4. Almost all of your science work *is, are* correct.

  5. One of your reports *is, are* excellent.

  6. All of your facts *is, are* correct.

  7. None of the information *is, are* easy to understand.

  8. Most of my classes *is, are* hard.

  9. None of my classes *is, are* easy.

  10. Almost all of my classes *is, are* interesting.

◇ PRACTICE 17. Indefinite pronouns. (Chart 14-6)
Directions: Complete the sentences with **nothing**, **anything**, **no one**, or **anyone**.

1. a. We didn't talk to _____anyone_____ at the park.
   b. We talked to _____no one_____ at the park.

2. a. I didn't see _____ special on the restaurant menu.
   b. I saw _____ special on the restaurant menu.

3. a. Robin brought home _____ to eat for dinner.
   b. Robin didn't bring home _____ to eat for dinner.

4. a. Ben didn't send e-mails to _____ today.
   b. Ben sent e-mails to _____ today.

◇ PRACTICE 18. Indefinite pronouns. (Chart 14-6)
Directions: Complete the sentences with **nothing**, **anything**, **no one**, or **anyone**.

1. I shopped at the mall for several hours, but I didn't buy _____anything_____.

2. I brought home _____ new to wear.

3. I had a quiet weekend. I didn't talk to _____.

   _____ called me.

4. I opened my lunch box, and there was _____ in it.

5. I ate _____ for lunch.

6. Is _____ in your class from a rural area?

7. Jill got a pet fish. She doesn't know _____ about fish.

8. She knows _____ about fish.

9. You can't tell _____ my secret.

10. Please promise to tell _____.

◇ PRACTICE 19. Indefinite pronouns. (Chart 14-7)
Directions: Complete the sentences with **something**, **someone**, **anything**, or **anyone**.

STATEMENT	NEGATIVE
1. He ate _____something_____.	He didn't eat _____.
2. She met _____.	She didn't meet _____anyone_____.

QUESTION

3. Did he eat _____? Did he eat _____?

4. Did she meet _____? Did she meet _____?

5. They spoke to _____.   They didn't speak to _____.

6. They bought _____.   They didn't buy _____.

QUESTION

7. Did they speak to _____?   Did they speak to _____?

8. Did they buy _____?   Did they buy _____?

◇ PRACTICE 20. Indefinite pronouns. (Chart 14-7)
   Directions: Complete the sentences with **something, someone, anything,** or **anyone.**

1. I didn't get _____*anything*_____ at the grocery store.

2. I didn't talk to _____ at the grocery store.

3. I bought _____ for you at the grocery store.

4. I met _____ from high school at the grocery store.

5. a. Did you buy _____ at the grocery store?

   b. Did you buy _____ at the grocery store?

6. a. Did you talk to _____ at the grocery store?

   b. Did you talk to _____ at the grocery store?

◇ PRACTICE 21. Indefinite pronouns. (Chart 14-7)
   Directions: Complete the sentences with **something, someone, anything,** or **anyone.**

1. A: Close your eyes. I have _____*something*_____ special for you.

   B: Oh, no! I forgot it was our anniversary. I don't have _____*anything*_____ for you.

2. A: Did the doctor give you _____ for your headaches?

   B: He did some tests. He didn't give me _____ yet.

3. A: I need to talk to _____ about my work schedule. Are you going to

      speak with _____ too?

   B: No, I'm not going to talk to _____.

4. A: I didn't see _____ from school on the bus today.

   B: A lot of people are absent. _____ got a cold, and now half of the
      class is sick.

5. A: Did you pick up _____ for dinner tonight?

   B: Sorry, I forgot. I didn't pick up _____.

6. A: I hear a loud noise. Maybe _____ is in the garage.

   B: I didn't hear _____. Are you sure?

   A: I'll look. Hmmm. I don't see _____ or _____ unusual.

◇ **PRACTICE 22. Subject-verb agreement with EVERY and ALL. (Chart 14-8)**
   Directions: Choose the correct completion for each sentence.

   1. All of the _____ are ready to graduate.
      A. student   (B.) students

   2. Every _____ in this room has worked hard.
      A. person   B. people

   3. All of the _____ in the store are for sale.
      A. shirt   B. shirts

   4. Are all of the _____ on sale too?
      A. sweater   B. sweaters

   5. Every _____ at this party likes to dance.
      A. teenager   B. teenagers

   6. Do all _____ like to dance?
      A. teenager   B. teenagers

   7. Every _____ in the world wants loving parents.
      A. child   B. children

   8. Do all _____ want to have children?
      A. parent   B. parents

◇**PRACTICE 23. Subject-verb agreement with EVERY and ALL. (Chart 14-8)**
   Directions: Choose the correct completion for each sentence.

   1. All of the teachers _____ tests every week.
      A. gives   (B.) give

   2. Everyone at this school _____ hard.
      A. studies   B. study

   3. _____ all of the students in your class participate in discussions?
      A. Does   B. Do

   4. _____ everyone in your class participate in discussions?
      A. Does   B. Do

   5. Not everybody in the class _____ to give their opinion.
      A. likes   B. like

6. All of the people in line _____ concert tickets.
     A. is buying   B. are buying

7. Everything is this room _____ from South America.
     A. is   B. are

8. Every child at the party _____ a present to take home.
     A. get   B. gets

9. _____ everything look okay?
     A. Does   B. Do

10. Everything _____ okay.
     A. looks   B. look

◇ PRACTICE 24. Error analysis. (Chart 14-8)
Directions: Check (✓) the incorrect sentences and correct them.

1. __✓__ Every ~~of the~~ teachers is on time.

2. _____ Every students is on time too.

3. _____ Everything in this room is very clean.

4. _____ Everything in the kitchen sink are dirty.

5. _____ Where does all of your friends live?

6. _____ Where was everyone when I called last night?

7. _____ Everybody in my family like dessert after dinner.

8. _____ Do everyone in your family likes dessert?

9. _____ Was everybody from your office at the wedding?

10. _____ Was all of the people at the wedding your friends?

11. _____ There are ten families in my apartment building. Everyone are friendly.

12. _____ Everything is okay.

◇ PRACTICE 25. Linking verbs + adjectives. (Chart 14-9)
Directions: Check (✓) the sentences that have a linking verb. <u>Underline</u> the linking verb.

1. __✓__ After it rains, the air <u>smells</u> very fresh.

2. _____ Your vacation plans sound interesting.

3. _____ The children are playing happily in the backyard.

4. _____ They like to run and climb trees.

5. _____ Does the vegetable soup taste good?

6. _____ The roses smell wonderful.

7. _____ They look beautiful, too.

8. _____ Jack looked for some flowers for his wife.

9. _____ Cindy went to bed early because she felt sick.

10. _____ White chocolate tastes very sweet. I love it.

◇ **PRACTICE 26. Linking verbs + adjectives. (Chart 14-9)**
   Directions: Complete each sentence with an appropriate adjective.

1. There's a new movie about space at the theater. I really want to go. It sounds

   _____ *interesting* _____ .

2. Carl woke up at 3:00 A.M., and never went back to sleep. He looked

   _____ this morning.

3. Mmmm. What are you baking? The kitchen smells _____ .

4. I got 100% on all my tests. I feel _____ .

5. Whew! Do you smell that smell? I think it's a skunk.

   It smells _____ .

6. I'm sorry, this chicken tastes _____ .
   I can't eat it.

7. The Smiths are having a beach party this weekend. It sounds _____ .
   Do you want to go?

8. A few hours after dinner, Ellen and Bill got sick. They felt _____ for
   the rest of the evening.

◇ **PRACTICE 27. Adverbs. (Chart 14-10)**
   Directions: Write the adverb forms for the given adjectives.

1. quiet   _____ *quietly* _____   8. careful   _____

2. clear   _____   9. quick   _____

3. neat   _____   10. slow   _____

4. correct   _____   11. late   _____

5. hard   _____   12. honest   _____

6. good   _____   13. fast   _____

7. early   _____   14. easy   _____

◇ PRACTICE 28. Adverbs. (Chart 14-10)
Directions: Complete each sentence with the adverb form of the given adjective.

1. *clear*   Our teacher explains everything _____clearly_____.

2. *easy*   This is a simple exercise. I can do it _____.

3. *late*   Spiro came to class _____.

4. *safe*   The plane arrived at the airport _____.

5. *fast*   Mike talks too _____. I can't understand him.

6. *hard*   Ms. Chan is a hard worker. She worked _____ all her life.

7. *good*   I didn't understand my co-worker's instructions very _____.

8. *honest*   Andrew's reasons for missing work were hard to believe. Did you

                _____ believe them?

9. *soft*   When the students became loud, the teacher spoke _____.

10. *careless* The driver _____ threw a cigarette out the car window and
                started a forest fire.

◇ PRACTICE 29. Linking verbs, adjectives, and adverbs. (Charts 14-9 and 14-10)
Directions: Complete the sentences with the adjective or adverb form of the given word.
Remember, adjectives, not adverbs, follow linking verbs.

1. *nervous*   Bill looked _____nervous_____.

                 He began his speech _____nervously_____.

                 His hands shook _____nervously_____.

2. *beautiful*   Rita dressed _____ for the party.

                 She looked _____.

                 She wears _____ clothes.

3. *good*   The flowers smell _____.

                 They grow _____ in this sunny garden.

4. *good*   Does the food taste _____?

                 Robert is a _____ cook.

5. *interesting* Your idea for the project sounds _____.

                 The project looks _____.

6. *bad* Anita wrote a _____ check at the store and gave it to the clerk.

She had no money in the bank, but she didn't feel _____ about doing that.

7. *fast* Tom drives _____.

He speaks _____, too.

◇ PRACTICE 30. Adjectives and adverbs. (Charts 14-9 and 14-10)
  Directions: Complete each sentence with the adjective or adverb form of the given word.

1. *clear* The teacher speaks ____*clearly*____. She gives

____*clear*____ examples.

2. *correct* You answered the question _____. That is the

_____ answer.

3. *late* I paid my phone bill _____. I don't like to make

_____ payments.

4. *beautiful* Look at the _____ pictures. The artist draws

_____.

5. *honest* Michael is an _____ child. He never lies. He answers

questions _____.

6. *beautiful* Rosa looked _____ on her wedding day. She is a

_____ girl.

7. *good* Mmmm. The food smells _____. I'm glad my

roommate is a _____ cook.

8. *easy* Isabelle writes _____ in English. Writing is an

_____ subject for her.

9. *good* The students swam _____. The team had a

_____ competition.

10. *quick* I need these copies _____. Is your copy machine

_____?

11. *sweet*   Candy tastes very _____. I love

_____ snacks.

12. *careless*   John is a _____ driver. Why does he drive so

_____?

◇ PRACTICE 31. Adjective and adverb review. (Charts 14-9 and 14-10)
     Directions: Complete each sentence with the correct form of the given adjective or adverb.

1. *slow*   This is a _____ *slow* _____ bus. I'm afraid we'll be late.

2. *slow*   There's a lot of traffic. The bus driver has to drive _____.

3. *hard*   The whole class studied _____ for the test.

4. *hard*   The teacher always gives _____ exams.

5. *clear*   The sky looks very _____ today.

6. *early*   The birds woke me up _____ this morning.

7. *fluent*   Jane speaks _____ French, but she can't speak English

_____.

8. *neat*   Your homework looks very _____.

9. *careful*   It's clear that you do your work _____.

10 *good*   The teacher said our group gave a _____ presentation.

11. *good*   She said we worked together _____.

CHART 14-A: SUMMARY: USES OF NOUNS

		NOUNS ARE USED AS
(a)	**NOUN** | ***Birds*** | fly. | subject verb	• subjects of a sentence, as in (a).
(b)	**NOUN** | Ken | opened | ***the door***. | subject verb object	• objects of a verb, as in (b).
(c)	**NOUN** | Birds | fly | in | ***the sky***. | subject verb prep. object of prep.	• objects of a preposition, as in (c).
(d)	**NOUN** | Yoko | is | ***a student***. | subject *be* noun complement	• noun complements* after ***be***, as in (d).
(e)	**NOUN + NOUN** I don't like ***winter*** weather.	• modifiers of other nouns, as in (e).

*A *complement* is a word that <u>completes</u> a sentence or a thought.

◇ **PRACTICE 32. Uses of nouns. (Chart 14-A)**

Directions: Underline the nouns. Then write the words above the correct grammatical descriptions.

A. A <u>kangaroo</u> is an <u>animal</u>.

B. My <u>wallet</u> is in my <u>pocket</u>.

1. | My wallet | is | in | my pocket. |
       subject   *be*   prep.   object of prep.

2. | A kangaroo | is | an animal. |
       subject   *be*   noun complement

C. Jason works in an office.

D. Karen held the baby in her arms.

E. Restaurants serve food.

3. |_____|_____|_____|
       subject   verb   object

4. |_____|_____|_____|_____|
       subject   verb   prep.   object of prep.

5. |_____|_____|_____|_____|_____|
       subject   verb   object   prep.   object of prep.

F. Korea is in Asia.

G. Korea is a peninsula.

6. |_____|_____|_____|_____|
       subject   *be*   prep.   object of prep.

7. |_____|_____|_____|
       subject   *be*   noun complement

H. Children play with toys.

I. Monkeys eat fruit.

J. Jack tied a string around the package.

8. |_____|_____|_____|
       subject   verb   object

9. |_____|_____|_____|_____|
       subject   verb   prep.   object of prep.

10. |_____|_____|_____|_____|_____|
       subject   verb   object   prep.   object of prep.

CHART 14-B: CONNECTED NOUNS: NOUN + *AND/OR* + NOUN

(a) |_**Birds**_ *and* _**airplanes**_ | fly. |
       NOUN + *and* + NOUN
      subject   verb
	And can connect two or more nouns.
	In (a): the subject = two nouns.
	In (b): the object = two nouns.
	In (c): the object = three nouns.

(b) | Ken | opened | *the **door** and the **window**.* |
  subject   verb   NOUN + *and* + NOUN
                       object
	Three (or more) nouns are separated by commas, as in (c). Two nouns, as in (a) and (b), are NOT separated by commas.

(c) | I | have | *a **book**, a **pen**, and a **pencil**.* |
  subject verb   NOUN + NOUN + *and* + NOUN
                     object	

(d) I'd like *some coffee* **or** *some tea.* NOUN + *or* + NOUN	*Or* can also connect two nouns, as in (d).

◇ PRACTICE 33. Connected nouns. (Chart 14-B)

Directions: <u>Underline</u> the connected nouns and circle how they are used.

1. You bought <u>apples</u> and <u>bananas</u>.
   a. subject
   (b.) object of a verb
   c. object of a preposition
   d. complement following *be*

2. I bought apples, bananas, and oranges.
   a. subject
   b. object of a verb
   c. object of a preposition
   d. complement following *be*

3. Jack and Olga bought bananas.
   a. subject
   b. object of a verb
   c. object of a preposition
   d. complement following *be*

4. Julia wants apples or bananas.
   a. subject
   b. object of a verb
   c. object of a preposition
   d. complement following *be*

5. Julia is at the market with Jack and Olga.
   a. subject
   b. object of a verb
   c. object of a preposition
   d. complement following *be*

6. Swimming and soccer are popular sports for kids.
   a. subject
   b. object of a verb
   c. object of a preposition
   d. complement following *be*

7. There are some books and magazines for you on the desk.
   a. subject
   b. object of a verb
   c. object of a preposition
   d. complement following *be*

8. Cars, trains, and trucks are kinds of vehicles.
   a. subject
   b. object of a verb
   c. object of a preposition
   d. complement following *be*

9. Do you prefer to travel in planes or trains?
   a. subject
   b. object of a verb
   c. object of a preposition
   d. complement following *be*

10. A tree has a trunk, branches, leaves, and roots.
    a. subject
    b. object of a verb
    c. object of a preposition
    d. complement following *be*

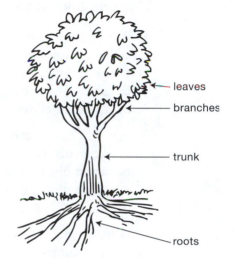

◇ PRACTICE 34. Using commas with connected nouns. (Chart 14-B)
   Directions: Add commas where necessary.

1. Ants, bees, and mosquitoes are insects.*

2. Ants and bees are insects. *(no change)*

3. Bears tigers and elephants are animals.

4. Bears and tigers are animals.

5. I bought some rice fruit and vegetables at the market.

6. I bought some rice and fruit at the market.

7. The three countries in North America are Canada the United States and Mexico.

---

*In a series of connected nouns, the comma immediately before *and* is optional. ALSO CORRECT: *Ants, bees and mosquitoes are insects.*

8. I read a lot of newspapers and magazines.

9. I had some soup and a sandwich for lunch.

10. Shelley had some soup a salad and a sandwich for lunch.

11. My favorite things in life are sunny days music good friends and books.

12. What do birds butterflies and airplanes have in common?

◇ PRACTICE 35. Uses of nouns and connected nouns. (Charts 14-A and 14-B)
Directions: Look at the underlined nouns. How are they used?

1. A <u>turtle</u> is a reptile.
   a. as a subject
   b. as an object of a verb
   c. as an object of a preposition
   d. as an adjective

2. A turtle has a hard <u>shell</u>.
   a. as a subject
   b. as an object of a verb
   c. as an object of a preposition
   d. as an adjective

3. A turtle pulls its <u>head</u>, <u>legs</u>, and <u>tail</u> into its shell.
   a. as a subject
   b. as an object of a verb
   c. as an object of a preposition
   d. as an adjective

4. Some turtles spend almost all of their lives in <u>water</u>.
   a. as a subject
   b. as an object of a verb
   c. as an object of a preposition
   d. as an adjective

5. Some turtles live on <u>land</u> for their entire lives.
   a. as a subject
   b. as an object of a verb
   c. as an object of a preposition
   d. as an adjective

6. <u>Baby</u> turtles face many dangers.
   a. as a subject
   b. as an object of a verb
   c. as an object of a preposition
   d. as an adjective

7. <u>Birds</u> and <u>fish</u> eat baby turtles.
   a. as a subject
   b. as an object of a verb
   c. as an object of a preposition
   d. as an adjective

8. Some green <u>sea</u> turtles live for 100 years.
   a. as a subject
   b. as an object of a verb
   c. as an object of a preposition
   d. as an adjective

9. Turtles face many dangers from <u>people</u>.
   a. as a subject
   b. as an object of a verb
   c. as an object of a preposition
   d. as an adjective

10. People replace beaches, forests, and other natural areas with <u>towns</u> and <u>farms</u>.
    a. as a subject
    b. as an object of a verb
    c. as an object of a preposition
    d. as an adjective

11. <u>People</u> poison natural areas with pollution.
    a. as a subject
    b. as an object of a verb
    c. as an object of a preposition
    d. as an adjective

12. Many <u>species</u> of turtles may not survive.
    a. as a subject
    b. as an object of a verb
    c. as an object of a preposition
    d. as an adjective

CHAPTER 15
Possessives

◇ **PRACTICE 1. Possessive nouns. (Chart 15-1)**
   Directions: Choose the meaning of each boldfaced noun: "one" or "more than one."

		HOW MANY?
1. My **friends'** parents are very friendly.	one	(more than one)
2. The **dog's** toys are all over the yard.	one	more than one

3. Where is your **parents'** house?	one	more than one
4. The **doctors'** offices are near the hospital.	one	more than one
5. The **doctor's** offices are near the hospital.	one	more than one
6. Our **co-worker's** schedule changes every week.	one	more than one
7. Your **daughters'** bedroom is very large.	one	more than one

◇ **PRACTICE 2. Possessive nouns. (Chart 15-1)**
   Directions: Complete the sentences with the correct nouns.

1. Jim's dog is active.

   The _____*dog*_____ belongs to _____*Jim*_____.

2. Bill's car is new.

   The _____ belongs to _____.

3. The teacher's desk is next to mine.

   The _____ belongs to _____.

4. The students' schedules are ready.

The _____ belong to _____.

5. I'm going to buy my parents' truck.

The _____ belongs to _____.

6. Where are the professors' offices?

The _____ belong to _____.

◇ PRACTICE 3. Possessive nouns (Chart 15-1)
   Directions: Add an apostrophe (') where necessary.

1. Where is Ben's grammar book?

2. Dans daughter is a university professor.

3. Who has the teachers pen?

4. My sisters baby doesn't sleep very much.

5. Dr. Smiths nurse is very helpful.

6. My pets names are Ping and Pong.

7. All our neighbors yards have flower and vegetable gardens.

8. What is your mothers maiden* name?

```
┌──────────────────────────────────────────────┐
│           APPLICATION FORM                     │
├──────────────────────────────────────────────┤
│ Name:    Sanchez,      Rosa           T        │
│          (last)        (first)    (middle initial) │
│ Address:  720 Lake Street, Green Hills, Texas  │
│ Phone number:  253 — 555 — 7063                │
│ Mother's maiden name: Santos                   │
└──────────────────────────────────────────────┘
```

◇ PRACTICE 4. Possessive nouns. (Chart 15-1)
   Directions: Add 's where necessary or Ø (nothing).

1. Tom __'s__ job is very interesting.

2. Tom __Ø__ works for a large airline.

3. Tom _____ buys airplanes.

4. Tom _____ wife, Olga, works at home.

5. Olga _____ designs Web pages.

6. Olga _____ is artistic.

7. Olga _____ Web sites are very creative.

---

*Maiden name is a married woman's last name (family name) before she got married.

◇ PRACTICE 5. Possessive nouns. (Chart 15-1)
Directions: Read the story. Then complete the sentences with the correct possessive name.

John   Jane

Mike   Marie   Belle   Ruff

Jane and John are married. They have one son and one daughter. Their son is Mike and their daughter is Marie. They also have two dogs: Belle and her puppy, Ruff.

1. Jane is _____John's_____ wife.

2. John is _____ husband.

3. Marie is _____ sister.

4. Belle is _____ mother.

5. Mike is _____ brother.

6. Ruff is _____ son.

7. Mike is Jane and _____ son.

8. Marie is John and _____ daughter.

◇ PRACTICE 6. Possessive noun or IS. (Chart 15-1)
Directions: Circle the meaning of 's: possessive or is.

1. Bob's happy.	possessive	(is)
2. Bob's bird sounds happy.	possessive	is
3. My teacher's not at school today.	possessive	is
4. The substitute teacher's nice.	possessive	is
5. Bill's manager went on vacation.	possessive	is
6. Bill's managing the office.	possessive	is

7. Bill's a good manager.   possessive   is

8. Bill's co-workers like him.   possessive   is

◇ **PRACTICE 7. Regular and irregular possessives. (Charts 15-1 and 15-2)**
   Directions: Circle the meaning of the boldfaced noun: "one" or "more than one."

		HOW MANY?
1. The **dogs'** food is in the yard.	one	(more than one)
2. The **cat's** dishes are in the garage.	one	more than one
3. The **teachers'** office is near the classrooms.	one	more than one
4. The **children's** toys are in the closet.	one	more than one
5. The **child's** toys are on the floor.	one	more than one
6. The **woman's** wallet fell out of her purse.	one	more than one
7. Where is the **women's** clothing department?	one	more than one
8. Is there a **men's** restroom nearby?	one	more than one
9. The **man's** children are waiting outside.	one	more than one

◇ **PRACTICE 8. Regular and irregular possessives. (Charts 15-1 and 15-2)**
   Directions: Make possessive phrases with the given words.

1. (one)   *boy \ truck*   the ___*boy's truck*_____

2. (five)   *boys \ trucks*   the ___*boys' trucks*_____

3. (three) *girls \ bikes*   the _____

4. (one)   *girl \ bike*   the _____

5. (three) *children \ toys*   the _____

6. (ten)   *students \ books*   the _____

7. (one)   *woman \ book*   the _____

8. (five)   *women \ books*   the _____

9. (two)   *people \ ideas*   some _____

10. (one)   *person \ ideas*   a _____

11. (two)   *men \ coats*   the _____

◇ **PRACTICE 9. Regular and irregular possessives. (Charts 15-1 and 15-2)**
Directions: Check (✓) the incorrect sentences and correct them.

1. ___✓___ The children's school is down the street.

2. _____ Several student's parents help at school.

3. _____ I have one brother. I like my brother's friends'.

4. _____ My brother's friend is very funny.

5. _____ I offered to fix my neighbor's computer.

6. _____ I like hearing other peoples' opinions.

7. _____ Womans' opinions are frequently different from men's opinions.

8. _____ Do you and your husband's agree very often?

◇ **PRACTICE 10. Personal pronouns. (Chart 15-3)**
Directions: Complete the sentences with the correct possessive pronoun (*mine, yours,* etc.) or possessive adjective (*my, your,* etc.).

1. It's his car. It's _____*his*_____.

2. It's her car. It's _____.

3. They're our cars. They're _____.

4. It's my car. It's _____.

5. It's your car. It's _____.

6. It's their car. It's _____.

7. The car belongs to her. It's _____*her*_____ car.

8. The car belongs to me. It's _____ car.

9. The car belongs to him. It's _____ car.

10. The car belongs to them. It's _____ car.

11. The car belongs to you. It's _____ car.

12. The car belongs to us. It's _____ car.

◇ **PRACTICE 11. WHOSE and WHO'S. (Chart 15-4)**
Directions: Choose the correct response for each sentence.

1. Whose are these?
   Ⓐ Pat's.   B. Pat.

2. Who's on the phone?
   A. Mr. Smith.   B. Mr. Smith's.

3. Who's coming?
   A. Some teachers.   B. Some teachers'.

4. Whose sweater is on the chair?
   A. Pam.   B. Pam's.

5. Who's going to help you with your homework?
   A. Andy.   B. Andy's.

6. Whose dictionary do you have?
   A. Mark.   B. Mark's.

7. Whose is this?
   A. My.   B. Mine.

◇ PRACTICE 12. WHOSE. (Chart 15-4)
   Directions: Make questions with **whose**.

   1. book \ this _____Whose book is this?_____

   2. glasses \ these _____

   3. toy \ this _____

   4. keys \ these _____

   5. shoes \ these _____

   6. shirt \ this _____

   7. cell phone \ this _____

   8. pens \ these _____

◇ PRACTICE 13. WHOSE and WHO'S. (Chart 15-4)
   Directions: Complete the sentences with **Whose** or **Who's**.

   1. ____Who's____ that?   6. _____ lunch is this?

   2. _____ is that?   7. _____ car is in the driveway?

   3. _____ coming?   8. _____ working tomorrow?

   4. _____ ready?   9. _____ outside?

   5. _____ glasses are these? 10. _____ work is this?

◇ **PRACTICE 14. WHOSE. (Chart 15-4)**
    Directions: Make sentences with the given words.

1. is \ pen \ that \ whose

    <u>   *Whose pen is that?*   </u>

2. whose \ are \ children \ those

3. who \ next \ is

4. are \ whose \ shoes \ on the floor

5. today \ absent \ is \ who

6. dictionary \ whose \ this \ is

◇ **PRACTICE 15. Review. (Charts 15-1 → 15-4)**
    Directions: Choose the correct completions.

1. This newspaper is yours. That newspaper is _____.
    A. our   Ⓑ ours   C. our's   D. ours'

2. My _____ name is Ernesto.
    A. father   B. fathers   C. fathers'   D. father's

3. _____ books are these?
    A. Who's   B. Whose   C. Who   D. Who are

4. _____ coming to the party?
    A. Who's   B. Whose   C. Who   D. Who are

5. I found two _____ backpacks in the park.
    A. girls   B. girl's   C. girl   D. girls'

6. My _____ are older than me.
    A. brother   B. brother's   C. brothers   D. brothers'

7. My _____ teacher is very patient.
    A. children's   B. childrens'   C. childs'   D. children

8. This is our hotel room and that room is _____.
    A. theirs'   B. their's   C. their   D. theirs

CHART 15-A: PERSONAL PRONOUN REVIEW

SUBJECT PRONOUNS	OBJECT PRONOUNS	POSSESSIVE PRONOUNS	POSSESSIVE ADJECTIVES
I	*me*	*mine*	*my* name(s)
you	*you*	*yours*	*your* name(s)
she	*her*	*hers*	*her* name(s)
he	*him*	*his*	*his* name(s)
it	*it*	*its*	*its* name(s)
we	*us*	*ours*	*our* name(s)
you	*you*	*yours*	*your* name(s)
they	*them*	*theirs*	*their* name(s)

(a) **We** saw an accident. (b) Anna saw **it** too. (c) I have my pen. Sue has **hers**. (d) **Her** pen is blue.	Personal pronouns are used as: • subjects, as in (a); • objects, as in (b); • OR to show possession, as in (c) and (d).
(e) I have a <u>book</u>. **It** is on my desk. (f) I have some <u>books</u>. **They** are on my desk.	Use a singular pronoun to refer to a singular noun. In (e): *book* and *it* are both singular. Use a plural pronoun to refer to a plural noun. In (f): *books* and *they* are both plural.
(g) **It's** sunny today. (h) I'm studying about India. I'm interested in **its** history. *INCORRECT: I'm interested in it's history.*	COMPARE: In (g): **it's** = *it is*. In (h): **its** = a possessive adjective: **its** history = **India's** history. A possessive adjective has NO apostrophe.

◇ PRACTICE 16. Pronoun review. (Chart 15-A)
    Directions: Choose the correct word in each sentence.

1. A: Where is (your,) yours bike?

   B: *Its, It's* near the school entrance. Where's *your, yours?*

   A: I can't remember!

2. A: Who left these building blocks on the floor?

   B: They're not *my, mine.*

   C: They're Mary's. I know they're *her, hers.*

   D: No, they're not. They're Tim's. He doesn't like to put away *his, him* toys.

3. A: My grammar class is easy. Sometimes *it's, its* too easy.

   B: *Our, Ours* isn't easy. *Our, Ours* class is really hard. I would like to have *your, yours* teacher.

   A: No, you wouldn't. *Her, She* lessons are kind of boring. She doesn't make *us, we* think very much.

4. A: Look! The dog is chasing *its, it's* tail.

   B: I know. *It's, Its* funny, isn't it?

5. A: Let's visit the Browns this weekend.

   B: Great idea! I'll call *they, them* to see if they'll be home.

   A: Ask *them, their* for *them, their* new address, too. They moved but kept *them, their* old phone number.

   B: Hmmm. I can't find my address book.* Do you have *your, yours?*

   A: Sure. Here it is.

◇ **PRACTICE 17. Pronoun and possessive adjective review. (Chart 15-A)**
   Directions: Complete each sentence with the correct pronoun or possessive adjective.

   1. A: Hi, Alice. This coat doesn't belong to me. Is it _____yours_____?

      B: No, it's not _____. Maybe it's Sara's. I'll go ask _____.

   2. A: There's Sue and John. Let's go talk to _____.

      B: I like Sue. I enjoy _____ a lot.

      A: I know John well. _____ works in my building. _____ office is next to mine. I see _____ a lot.

   3. A: Does this cat belong to your next-door neighbors?

      B: No, she isn't _____. Maybe she is Mr. Brown's cat. I'll call _____.

      A: She looks hungry. Can you give _____ some milk?
      B: Sure.

   4. A: Whose English-English dictionary is this? Joan, is it _____?

      B: It looks like _____, but _____ dictionary has my name on it.
      A: Hmmm. There's no name on it.

      B: There's a group of students over there. I'll ask _____. Excuse me, is this dictionary _____?

   _____
   *address book = a small book for a person to write phone numbers and addresses.

5. A: My husband and I like to travel a lot. _____ are going to Nepal for

_____ next vacation.

B: That sounds very interesting. How long will _____ stay there?

A: Three weeks. _____ husband has a one-month vacation.

B: My husband and I have trouble scheduling vacations together. _____
vacations are in different months of the year.

A: I'm glad _____ are always at the same time. We feel lucky.

CHART 15-B: APOSTROPHE REVIEW

(a) **I'm** happy. (*INCORRECT*: *I'am happy.*) **She's** happy. **We're** happy.	USES OF THE APOSTROPHE • With contractions of pronouns and **am, is,** and **are.** See Chart 1-4.
(b) **Bill's** happy.	• With contractions of nouns and **is.** In (b), **Bill's** = *Bill is.* *
(c) **That's** my notebook.	• With the contraction of **that** and **is.**
(d) **There's** a book on the table. **There're** some books on the table.	• With the contractions of **there** and **is/are.**
(e) **What's** this? **Where's** Anna?	• With contractions of some question words and **is.**
(f) **Who's** that? → It's *Mike.*	COMPARE In (f): **Who's** = *who is.*
(g) **Whose** is that? → It's *Mike's.*	In (g): **Whose** = a question word that asks about possession. It has NO apostrophe.
(h) Tina **isn't** here.	• With negative contractions: **isn't, aren't, wasn't, weren't, doesn't, don't, won't, can't.**
(i) **Bill's** hair is brown.	• With possessive nouns, as in (i) and (j). See Charts 15-1 and 15-2.
(j) My **parents'** house is white.	
(k) This pen belongs to Ann. It is **hers.**	Apostrophes are NOT used with possessive pronouns. In (l): *hers* with an apostrophe (*her's*) is NEVER correct.
(l) *INCORRECT*: *It is her's.*	

*Nouns are regularly contracted with **is** in spoken English. In written English, contractions of a noun and **is** (e.g., *Bill's happy*) are found in informal English (for example, in a letter to a friend), but not in formal English (for example, an academic paper). In general, verb contractions (*I'm, you're, isn't, there's,* etc.) are found in informal English, but not used in very formal English.

◇ PRACTICE 18. Apostrophe review. (Chart 15-B)

Directions: Add apostrophes where necessary.

1. That's Ann's book.

2. That book is hers. *(no change)*

3. Jims car is small.

4. Jims in New York this week.

5. Hes visiting his brother.

6. Im a little hungry this morning.

7. Tonys my neighbor.

8. Tonys apartment is next to mine.

9. Whos that woman?

10. Shes Bobs wife.

11. Whose book is that?

12. Is it yours?

13. Its Ginas book.

14. Wheres your dictionary?

15. Amy wont go to the movie with us. She doesnt have enough money.

16. Paris is a popular tourist destination. Its most famous attraction is the Eiffel Tower. Its most famous building is the Louvre Museum. Its also famous for its night life.

◇ PRACTICE 19. Apostrophe review. (Chart 15-B)
Directions: Add apostrophes where necessary.

1. Yoko's last name is Yakamoto.

2. Yokos a student in my English class.

3. Pablo is a student. Hes in my class. His last name is Alvarez.

4. Pablos full name is Pablo Alvarez.

5. Youre a student. Your name is Ali.

6. Im a student. I am in Mr. Lees English class.

7. Mary and Anita have purses. Marys purse is black. Anitas purse is brown.

8. Marys in class today. Anitas at home.

9. Whose books are these? This book is mine. Thats yours.

10. Whats wrong? Whats happening? Whos that man? Wheres he going?

11. Im looking at a book. Its a grammar book. Its cover is red. Its on my desk. Its open. Its title is *Basic English Grammar.*

12. Theres a bird in the tree. Its black and red. Its chest is red. Its wings, tail, and back are black. Its sitting on a branch.

13. People admire the tiger for its beauty and strength. Its a magnificent animal. Unfortunately, its survival as a species is in doubt. Its an endangered species. There are very few tigers in the world today.

◇ PRACTICE 20. Error analysis: pronoun review. (Charts 15-A and 15-B)
Directions: Correct the errors in pronoun usage.

Dear Heidi,

                                                          my
(1)   Everything is going fine. I like ~~mine~~ new apartment very much. Its large

(2)   and comfortable. I like me roommate too. Him name is Alberto. You will meet

(3)   them when your visit I next month. His from Colombia. His studying English

(4)   too. Were classmates. We were classmates last semester too. We share the rent

(5)   and the utility bills, but us don't share the telephone bill. He pays for his's calls

(6)   and my pay for my. He's telephone bill is very high because he has a girlfriend

(7)   in Colombia. He calls she often. Sometimes her calls he. Them talk on the

(8)   phone a lot.

(9)   Ours neighbors are Mr. and Mrs. Black. Their very nice. We talk to it

(10)   often. Ours apartment is next to their. Theirs have a three-year-old* daughter.

(11)   Shes really cute. Hers name is Joy. Them also have a cat. Its black and white.

(12)   Its eyes are yellow. Its name is Whiskers. Its a friendly cat. Sometimes they're

(13)   cat leaves a dead mouse outside ours door.

(14)   I'am looking forward to you're visit.

Love, Carl

---

*NOTE: When a person's age is used as an adjective in front of a noun, the word *year* is singular (NOT plural) and hyphens (-) are used: *a three-year-old daughter.*
  INCORRECT: *They have a three years old daughter.*
  CORRECT: *They have a three-year-old daughter.* OR: *Their daughter is three years old.*

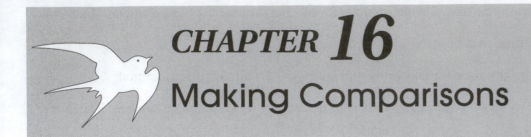

CHAPTER 16
Making Comparisons

◇ **PRACTICE 1. THE SAME (AS), SIMILAR (TO), DIFFERENT (FROM).** (Chart 16-1)
   Directions: Complete the sentences with the correct preposition (*to, as, from*) or Ø.

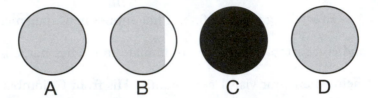

A   B   C   D

1. A and D are the same _____Ø_____.

2. A is the same _____ D.

3. A and C are different _____.

4. A and B are similar _____.

5. A is different _____ C.

6. A is similar _____ B.

7. B and D are similar _____.

8. C and D are different _____.

◇ **PRACTICE 2. THE SAME (AS), SIMILAR (TO), DIFFERENT (FROM).** (Chart 16-1)
   Directions: Complete the sentences using *the same (as), similar (to), or different (from)*.

1   2   3   4

1. 4 is ___*the same as*___ 1.

2. 1 and 4 are ___*the same*___ .

3. 1 and 2 are _____ .

4. 2 and 4 are _____ .

5. 2 and 3 are _____ .

6. 1 is _____ 2.

7. 2 is _____ 3.

8. 4 is _____ 2.

9. 1 and 3 are _____ .

10. 3 is _____ 4.

◇ **PRACTICE 3. THE SAME (AS), SIMILAR (TO), DIFFERENT (FROM). (Chart 16-1)**
   Directions: Make sentences using the given words.

   1. English / Japanese

      (different)   _____English is different from Japanese._____

      (different from)   _____English and Japanese are different._____

   2. trains / buses

      (similar)   _____

      (similar to)   _____

   3. your grammar book / my grammar book

      (the same as) _____

      (the same)   _____

   4. women / men

      (different)   _____

      (different from) _____

◇ **PRACTICE 4. LIKE and ALIKE. (Chart 16-2)**
   Directions: Complete the sentences with *like* or *alike*.

   1. A pen is _____ *like* _____ a pencil.

   2. Pens and pencils are _____.

   3. Highways and freeways are _____.

   4. A freeway is _____ a highway.

   5. The Pacific Ocean and Atlantic Ocean are _____.

   6. A mouse is _____ a rat.

   7. A mouse isn't _____ an elephant.

   8. Hands and feet are _____.

   9. Are people around the world _____?

◇ **PRACTICE 5. LIKE and ALIKE. (Chart 16-2)**
Directions: Complete the sentences with ***like*** or ***alike*** and a word from the list. Then explain why they are alike.

dark chocolate	milkshakes	physics
doctors	newspapers	Thailand
knives		

1. *like*   Nurses _____ are like doctors. They help people. _____

2. *alike*   White chocolate _____

3. *like*   Magazines _____

4. *alike*   Scissors _____

5. *alike*   Malaysia _____

6. *like*   Ice-cream cones _____

7. *alike*   Chemistry _____

◇ **PRACTICE 6. Comparative form. (Chart 16-3)**
Directions: Write the comparative form for each adjective.

1. *young*   _____ younger than _____

2. *wide*   _____

3. *cheap*   _____

4. *dark*   _____

5. *smart*   _____

6. *old*   _____

7. *happy*   _____

8. *important*   _____

9. *difficult*   _____

10. *expensive*   _____

11. *easy*   _____

12. *funny*   _____

13. *good*   _____

14. *far*   _____

15. *fat*   _____

16. *hot*   _____

17. *thin*   _____

18. *bad*   _____

◇ PRACTICE 7. Comparatives. (Chart 16-3)

Directions: Complete the sentences. Use the comparative form of the given words.

1. *warm*   The weather today is ___*warmer than*___ it was yesterday.

2. *funny*   This story is _____ that story.

3. *interesting*   This book is _____ that book.

4. *smart*   Joe is _____ his brother.

5. *famous*   A movie star is _____ I am.

6. *wide*   A highway is _____ an alley.

7. *large*   Your apartment is _____ mine.

8. *dark*   Tom's mustache is _____ Dan's.

9. *good*   My wife's cooking is _____ mine.

10. *bad*   My cooking is _____ my wife's.

11. *pretty*   This dress is _____ that one.

12. *confusing*   This story is _____ that story.

13. *far*   My house is _____ from downtown _____

                   your house is.

14. *good*   Reading a good book is _____ watching television.

15. *easy*   My English class is _____ my history class.

16. *beautiful*   A flower is _____ a weed.

weed

◇ PRACTICE 8. Comparatives. (Chart 16-3)
Directions: Compare the two culture classes using the given words. Give your own opinions.

Student Rating	
Culture 101 A	★ ★ ★ ★ ★
Culture 101 B	★ ★

CULTURE CLASSES

Classes	101 A	101 B
Teaching style	discussions/games/movies	lecture
Student rating*	5/5	2/5
Homework	3 times/week	every day
Tests	3/term	every week
Average student grade	90%	75%

1. *interesting* _____ 101A is more interesting than 101B. _____

2. *boring* _____

3. *hard* _____

4. *easy* _____

5. *popular* _____

6. *difficult* _____

7. *enjoyable* _____

_____

*rating = 5 (excellent); 1 (bad).

◇ PRACTICE 9. Comparatives. (Chart 16-3)

Directions: Compare the three places. Write comparative sentences using the given words.
Give your own opinion.

| country | city | suburbs |

Life in the . . .

1. *quiet*

   _____Life in the country is quieter than life in the city._____

2. *expensive*

   _____

3. *relaxing*

   _____

4. *busy*

   _____

5. *convenient*

   _____

6. *beautiful*

   _____

7. *cheap*

   _____

8. *nice*

   _____

9. *safe*

   _____

10. *good*

   _____

◇ **PRACTICE 10. Comparative and superlative forms. (Charts 16-3 and 16-4)**
   Directions: Write both the comparative and superlative form of the given words.

	COMPARATIVE	SUPERLATIVE
1. expensive	*more expensive than*	*the most expensive*
2. lazy		
3. clean		
4. old		
5. young		
6. new		
7. beautiful		
8. exciting		
9. nice		
10. quiet		
11. bad		
12. fat		
13. thin		
14. hot		
15. good		
16. cheap		
17. far		

◇ **PRACTICE 11. Superlatives. (Chart 16-4)**
   Directions: Complete the sentences using superlatives. Give your opinion.

   1. *hard subject in high school*

      The ___*hardest subject in high school is calculus.*___

   2. *beautiful city in the world*

      The _____

   3. *interesting show on TV*

      The _____

4. *boring sport to watch*

The _____

5. *easy language to learn*

The _____

6. *talented movie star*

The _____

7. *relaxing place to go for vacation*

The _____

8. *good place to live*

The _____

◇ PRACTICE 12. Superlatives. (Chart 16-4)

Directions: Compare the three places to eat. Use the words in the list. Write superlative sentences using the given words. Give your own opinion.

> *a fast-food restaurant*
> *a 5-star restaurant*
> *an Internet café*

1. *expensive*   *A 5-star restaurant is the most expensive.*

2. *convenient* _____

3. *relaxing* _____

4. *busy* _____

5. *nice* _____

6. *interesting* _____

7. *popular* _____

8. *quiet* _____

9. *cheap* _____

10. *useful* _____

◇ PRACTICE 13. Review: comparatives and superlatives. (Charts 16-3 and 16-4)
Directions: Write sentences using comparatives and superlatives. Use the given information.

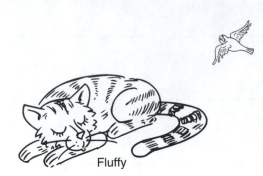  

Fluffy   Rex   Polly

15 lbs/7 kilos
likes to sleep all day
black and white fur
2 years old

70 lbs/32 kilos
likes to chase birds and hunt
brown fur
7 years old

1 ounce/.03 kilos
likes to sing and look around
blue and yellow feathers
10 years old

1. *lazy*   ___Fluffy is the laziest.___

  ___Fluffy is lazier than Rex.___

2. *active* _____

  _____

3. *young*   _____

  _____

4. *heavy*   _____

  _____

5. *colorful* _____

  _____

6. *big*   _____

  _____

7. *old*   _____

     _____

8. *small*   _____

     _____

9. *light**   _____

     _____

◇ PRACTICE 14. ONE OF + superlative + plural noun. (Chart 16-5)
    Directions: Complete each sentence with the correct form of the given adjective and noun.

   1. *hot \ month*   August is one of _____*the hottest months*_____ in my

                                    hometown.

   2. *fast \ car*   A Ferrari is one of _____ in the

                                      world.

   3. *happy \ couple*   Ted and Sue are one of _____

                                      in our neighborhood.

   4. *funny \ child*   Ricky is one of _____ in my class.

   5. *good \ teacher*   Ann Jones is one of _____

                                      at my school.

   6. *tall \ woman*   Donna is one of _____

                                      in our class.

   7. *old \ man*   Ken is one of _____ in our class.

   8. *interesting \ person*   Dan is one of _____

                                      in our office.

   9. *scary \ animal*   A crocodile is one of _____

                                      in the world.

_____

*_light_ = opposite of *heavy*.

◇ PRACTICE 15. ONE OF + superlative + plural noun. (Chart 16-5)

Directions: Make sentences with **one of** + superlative. Use the given adjectives and the sports in the list. Give your own opinion.

baseball	karate	skydiving
boxing	race-walking	soccer
golf	skiing	swimming

1. *easy sport to learn*   <u>Running is one of the easiest sports to learn.</u>

2. *dangerous*

3. *expensive*

4. *safe*

5. *difficult*

6. *interesting*

7. *good sport for your heart*

◇ PRACTICE 16. ONE OF + superlative. (Chart 16-5)

Directions: Make sentences with **one of** + superlative. Use the given words. Give your own opinion.

1. small \ country

  <u>Lichtenstein is one of the smallest countries</u>   in the world.

2. big \ city

3. hard \ language to learn

_____ .

4. interesting \ place to visit

_____ .

5. pretty \ place to visit

_____ .

6. expensive \ city

_____ to visit.

7. important \ person

_____ in the world.

◇ PRACTICE 17. Review: comparatives, superlatives, and ONE OF. (Charts 16-3 → 16-5)
Directions: Complete the sentences with the correct form of the given words.

1. *big*   Asia is _____ *the biggest* _____ continent in the world.

2. *long*   The Nile is _____ the Amazon.

3. *hot \ place*   The Sahara Desert is one of _____ in the world.

4. *cold \ place*   The Arctic Circle is one of _____ in the world.

5. *large*   Is Canada _____ than Russia?

6. *large*   Russia is _____ country in the world.

7. *long*   The femur (thigh bone) is _____ bone in our body.

femur →

8. *small*   _____ bone in our body is in the ear. It is called the stirrup bone.

9. *scary*   What do you think is _____ animal in the world?

10. *dangerous \ animal* The hippopotamus is one of _____ in the world.

◇ **PRACTICE 18. Using BUT. (Chart 16-6)**

Directions: Complete each sentence with the opposite adjective.

1. A sports car is fast, but a bike is _____*slow*_____.

2. The sun is hot, but the moon is _____.

3. Mr. Benton is an easy teacher, but Mrs. Benton is a _____ teacher.

4. Building a paper airplane is simple, but building a real airplane is _____.

5. A giraffe has a long neck, but a rabbit has a _____ neck.

6. Real diamonds are expensive, but fake diamonds are _____.

7. A hard pillow is uncomfortable, but a soft pillow is _____.

8. Red is a warm color, but blue is a _____ color.

9. Feathers are light, but rocks are _____.

10. The wheel is an old invention, but the car is a _____ invention.

◇ **PRACTICE 19. Verbs after BUT. (Chart 16-7)**

Directions: Complete each sentence with an appropriate verb: affirmative or negative.

1. Fried foods are greasy, but boiled foods _____*aren't*_____.

2. Cars can't fly, but planes _____.

3. Children often don't like vegetables, but adults generally _____.

4. Warm baths feel relaxing, but cold baths _____.

5. A warm bath feels relaxing, but a cold bath _____.

6. The students were in class yesterday, but their teacher _____.

7. Susan won't be at the party, but her husband _____.

8. I don't like fish, but my husband _____.

9. Ralph studied hard, but Daniel _____.

10. Newborn babies sleep most of the day, but adults usually _____.

11. Billy isn't a hard worker, but his brother _____.

12. A few students in the class can understand the math problems, but I _____.

13. Dr. Jones will work this weekend, but his partner _____.

14. The English books aren't in the bookstore, but the science books _____.

15. Mark wasn't on time for class, but Gary _____.

16. Mark didn't arrive on time, but Gary _____.

17. Electric cars are quiet, but diesel cars _____.

◇ **PRACTICE 20. Verbs after BUT.** (Chart 16-7)
Directions: Complete the sentences with your own words.

1. Birds have wings, but _____*cats don't.*_____

2. Dogs barks, but _____

3. Fish can stay underwater for a long time, but _____

4. Skunks don't smell good, but _____

5. The weather in the desert is hot, but _____

6. Expensive things aren't important, but _____

7. Happiness is important, but _____

8. It (was/wasn't) cold yesterday, but today it _____

◇ **PRACTICE 21. Comparisons with adverbs.** (Charts 16-8 and 14-10)
Directions: Write the correct form for the given adjectives.

	ADJECTIVE	ADVERB	COMPARATIVE	SUPERLATIVE
1.	quick	*quickly*	*more quickly*	*the most quickly*
2.	clear			
3.	slow			
4.	beautiful			
5.	neat			
6.	careful			
7.	fluent			
8.	good			
9.	hard			
10.	early			
11.	late			
12.	fast			

◇ PRACTICE 22. Adverbs: comparatives and superlatives. (Chart 16-8)
   Directions: Complete the sentences with the correct form (comparative or superlative) of the given adverbs.

   1. *beautifully*   The art students draw ____*more beautifully than*____ their teacher.

   2. *carefully*   Rob drives _____ his brother.

   3. *quickly*   Ted finished the test _____ of all.

   4. *hard*   Who works _____ in your class?

   5. *late*   The bride arrived at her wedding _____ the guests.

   6. *early*   The groom arrived _____ of all.

   7. *good*   Tina can swim _____ Tom.

   8. *quickly*   Ana learns math _____ her classmates.

   9. *slowly*   My grandfather walks _____ my grandmother.

   10. *fluently*   Ben speaks English _____ of all the students.

   11. *fast*   Ben learns languages _____ his classmates.

   12. *good*   Sam can dive _____ of all.

◇ PRACTICE 23. Adjectives and adverbs: comparatives and superlatives.
         (Charts 16-3, 16-4, and 16-8)
   Directions: Write the correct form of the given adjectives.

   1. *heavy*   This suitcase is ____*heavier than*____ that one.

   2. *dangerous*   A motorcycle is _____ a bicycle.

   3. *dangerous*   Tom drives _____ Fred.

   4. *dangerous*   Steven drives _____ of all.

   5. *clear*   Pedro speaks _____ Ernesto.

6. *clear*   Our pronunciation teacher is _____ our grammar teacher.

7. *clear*   She speaks _____ of all.

8. *hard*   Sue studies _____ Fred.

9. *hard*   Jean studies _____ of all.

10. *good*   My son can play the piano _____ I can.

11. *good*   My mother can play the piano _____ of all.

12. *good*   I like the guitar _____ the piano.

13. *long*   My husband's work days are _____ his co-workers.

14. *long*   His work days are _____ of all.

15. *neat*   Mrs. Bell looks _____ Mr. Bell.

16. *neat*   Mrs. Bell dresses _____ Mr. Bell.

◇ **PRACTICE 24. Chapter review.**

   Directions: Choose the correct completion for each sentence.

   1. Dolphins and whales are _____ .
      (A.) similar   B. like   C. the same   D. different from

   2. The weather in Canada is _____ the weather in Mexico.
      A. coolest   B. cooler than   C. the coolest   D. more cool than

   3. What is your _____ color?
      A. more favorite   B. the most favorite   C. favorite   D. more favorite than

   4. Men are _____ women.
      A. different from   B. different as   C. different   D. different to

   5. We live _____ from town than you do.
      A. far   B. more far   C. farthest   D. farther

6. Is happiness _____ money?
   A. importanter than
   C. important
   B. more important than
   D. more important

7. The weather is cold today, but yesterday it _____.
   A. isn't
   B. doesn't
   C. wasn't
   D. didn't

8. I have _____ you.
   A. a same shirt
   B. same shirt
   C. the same shirt as
   D. same shirt as

9. The Atlantic Ocean isn't _____ ocean in the world.
   A. a biggest
   B. the biggest
   C. a big
   D. bigger than

10. Alison and Jeff don't study in the library, but Kathy _____.
    A. does
    B. doesn't
    C. isn't
    D. is

11. I thought the math test was hard, but my friends thought it was _____.
    A. easy
    B. difficult
    C. easier
    D. hardest

12. I thought it was one of _____ of the year.
    A. the hard test
    B. a hard tests
    C. a hard test
    D. the hardest tests

APPENDIX **1**
Irregular Verbs

SIMPLE FORM	SIMPLE PAST	SIMPLE FORM	SIMPLE PAST
be	was, were	keep	kept
become	became	know	knew
begin	began	leave	left
bend	bent	lend	lent
bite	bit	lose	lost
blow	blew	make	made
break	broke	meet	met
bring	brought	pay	paid
build	built	put	put
buy	bought	read	read
catch	caught	ride	rode
choose	chose	ring	rang
come	came	run	ran
cost	cost	say	said
cut	cut	see	saw
do	did	sell	sold
draw	drew	send	sent
drink	drank	shake	shook
drive	drove	shut	shut
eat	ate	sing	sang
fall	fell	sit	sat
feed	fed	sleep	slept
feel	felt	speak	spoke
fight	fought	spend	spent
find	found	stand	stood
fly	flew	steal	stole
forget	forgot	swim	swam
get	got	take	took
give	gave	teach	taught
go	went	tear	tore
grow	grew	tell	told
hang	hung	think	thought
have	had	throw	threw
hear	heard	understand	understood
hide	hid	wake up	woke up
hit	hit	wear	wore
hold	held	win	won
hurt	hurt	write	wrote

APPENDIX 2
The English Alphabet

A	a		N	n
B	b		O	o
C	c		P	p
D	d		Q	q
E	e		R	r
F	f		S	s
G	g		T	t
H	h		U	u
I	i		V	v
J	j		W	w
K	k		X	x
L	l		Y	y
M	m		Z	z★

Vowels = *a, e, i, o u.*
Consonants = *b, c, d, f, g, h, j, k, l, m, n, p, q, r, s, t, v, w, x, y, z.*

★The letter *z* is pronounced "zee" in American English and "zed" in British English.

APPENDIX 3
Numbers

CARDINAL NUMBERS

1	one
2	two
3	three
4	four
5	five
6	six
7	seven
8	eight
9	nine
10	ten
11	eleven
12	twelve
13	thirteen
14	fourteen
15	fifteen
16	sixteen
17	seventeen
18	eighteen
19	nineteen
20	twenty
21	twenty-one
22	twenty-two
23	twenty-three
24	twenty-four
25	twenty-five
26	twenty-six
27	twenty-seven
28	twenty-eight
29	twenty-nine
30	thirty
40	forty
50	fifty
60	sixty
70	seventy
80	eighty
90	ninety
100	one hundred
200	two hundred
1,000	one thousand
10,000	ten thousand
100,000	one hundred thousand
1,000,000	one million

ORDINAL NUMBERS

1st	first
2nd	second
3rd	third
4th	fourth
5th	fifth
6th	sixth
7th	seventh
8th	eighth
9th	ninth
10th	tenth
11th	eleventh
12th	twelfth
13th	thirteenth
14th	fourteenth
15th	fifteenth
16th	sixteenth
17th	seventeenth
18th	eighteenth
19th	nineteenth
20th	twentieth
21st	twenty-first
22nd	twenty-second
23rd	twenty-third
24th	twenty-fourth
25th	twenty-fifth
26th	twenty-sixth
27th	twenty-seventh
28th	twenty-eighth
29th	twenty-ninth
30th	thirtieth
40th	fortieth
50th	fiftieth
60th	sixtieth
70th	seventieth
80th	eightieth
90th	ninetieth
100th	one hundredth
200th	two hundredth

APPENDIX 4

Days of the Week and Months of the Year

DAYS

Monday	(Mon.)
Tuesday	(Tues.)
Wednesday	(Wed.)
Thursday	(Thurs.)
Friday	(Fri.)
Saturday	(Sat.)
Sunday	(Sun.)

MONTHS

January	(Jan.)
February	(Feb.)
March	(Mar.)
April	(Apr.)
May	(May)
June	(June)
July	(July)
August	(Aug.)
September	(Sept.)
October	(Oct.)
November	(Nov.)
December	(Dec.)

Using numbers to write the date:

month/day/year
10/31/41 = October 31, 1941
4/15/92 = April 15, 1992
7/4/1906 = July 4, 1906
7/4/07 = July 4, 2007

Saying dates:

USUAL WRITTEN FORM	USUAL SPOKEN FORM
January 1	January first/the first of January
March 2	March second/the second of March
May 3	May third/the third of May
June 4	June fourth/the fourth of June
August 5	August fifth/the fifth of August
October 10	October tenth/the tenth of October
November 27	November twenty-seventh/the twenty-seventh of November

APPENDIX 5
Ways of Saying Time

9:00	It's nine o'clock. It's nine.
9:05	It's nine-oh-five. It's five (minutes) after nine. It's five (minutes) past nine.
9:10	It's nine-ten. It's ten (minutes) after nine. It's ten (minutes) past nine.
9:15	It's nine-fifteen. It's a quarter after nine. It's a quarter past nine.
9:30	It's nine-thirty. It's half past nine.
9:45	It's nine-forty-five. It's a quarter to ten. It's a quarter of ten.
9:50	It's nine-fifty. It's ten (minutes) to ten. It's ten (minutes) of ten.
12:00	It's noon. It's midnight.

A.M. = morning   It's nine A.M.
P.M. = afternoon/evening/night   It's nine P.M.

APPENDIX 6

Two-Syllable Verbs: Spelling of *-ED* and *-ING*

	VERB	SPEAKING STRESS
(a)	visit	**VIS** · it
(b)	admit	ad · **MIT**

Some verbs have two syllables. In (a): *visit* has two syllables: *vis + it*. In the word *visit*, the stress is on the first syllable. In (b): the stress is on the second syllable in the word *admit*.

	VERB	STRESS	*-ED* FORM	*-ING* FORM
(c)	visit	**VIS** · it	visited	visiting
(d)	open	**O** · pen	opened	opening
(e)	admit	ad · **MIT**	admitted	admitting
(f)	occur	oc · **CUR**	occurred	occurring

For two-syllable verbs that end in a vowel and a consonant:
- The consonant is not doubled if the stress is on the first syllable, as in (c) and (d).
- The consonant is doubled if the stress is on the second syllable, as in (e) and (f).

COMMON VERBS

Stress on first syllable:

VERB	STRESS	*-ED* FORM	*-ING* FORM
answer	**AN** · swer	answered	answering
happen	**HAP** · pen	happened	happening
listen	**LIS** · ten	listened	listening
offer	**OF** · fer	offered	offering
enter	**EN** · ter	entered	entering

Stress on second syllable:

VERB	STRESS	*-ED* FORM	*-ING* FORM
prefer	pre · **FER**	preferred	preferring
permit	per · **MIT**	permitted	permitting
refer	re · **FER**	referred	referring
begin	be · **GIN**	(no *-ed* form)	beginning

Index

Answer Key

To the student: To make it easy to correct your answers, remove this answer key along the perforations and make a separate answer key booklet for yourself.

Chapter 9: EXPRESSING PAST TIME, PART 2

◇ **PRACTICE 1, p. 128.**

Order may vary.
1. Where did Rosa go? (She went) to Nairobi.
2. What time/When did she leave? (She left) at 2 P.M.
3. Why did she go there? (She went) for business.
4. Where did Oscar go? (He went) to Mexico City.
5. Why did he go there? (He went) to visit family.
6. When did he leave? (He left) on March 22.

◇ **PRACTICE 2, p. 129.**

1. B   3. E   5. D
2. F   4. C   6. A

◇ **PRACTICE 3, p. 129.**

1. Where did you study last night?
2. When/What time did you leave the library?
3. Why did you leave the library?
4. Where did you and your friends go yesterday afternoon?
5. Where did you get your sandals?
6. Why was Bobby in bed?
7. Why was Bobby sick?
8. When did Sandra get back from Brazil?

◇ **PRACTICE 4, p. 129.**

Answers may vary.
1. Why didn't you call?
2. Why didn't you come?
3. Why didn't you ask for help?
4. Why didn't you do your homework?
5. Why didn't you go shopping?
6. Why didn't you clean it / your bedroom?

◇ **PRACTICE 5, p. 130.**

1. What did you buy?
2. Did you buy a digital camera?
3. What did you study?
4. Did you study math?
5. What are they looking at?
6. Are they looking at a map?
7. What did you dream about last night?

8. Is she interested in science?
9. What is she interested in?
10. What did David talk about?
11. Did David talk about his country?
12. What are you thinking about?
13. What does *nothing in particular* mean?
14. What are you afraid of?

◇ **PRACTICE 6, p. 131.**

1. a. the police?
   b. Julie call?
2. a. Sara?
   b. the children visit?
3. a. Janet help?
   b. the new manager? Janet.
4. a. the advanced students?
   b. Professor Jones teach? The advanced students.
5. a. the police catch? The thief.
   b. the thief? The police.
6. a. a monster? Tommy.
   b. Tommy dream about? A monster.

◇ **PRACTICE 7, p. 132.**

1. a. Who helped Judy?
   b. Who did Ron help?
2. a. Who did the doctor examine?
   b. Who examined the patient?
3. a. Who called the supervisor?
   b. Who did Miriam call?
4. a. Who surprised the teacher?
   b. Who did the students surprise?
5. a. Who did Andrew and Catherine wait for?
   b. Who waited for Mrs. Allen?

◇ **PRACTICE 8, p. 132.**

1. Who did you see?
2. Who did you talk to?
3. Who did you visit?
4. Who answered the question?
5. Who taught the English class?
6. Who helped you?
7. Who did you help?
8. Why carried your suitcase?
9. Who called?

◇ **PRACTICE 9, p. 133.**

1. Who gave an anniversary party? Ray gave an anniversary party.
2. Who did Ray give a party for? He gave a party for his parents.
3. Who gave a New Year's party? Dr. Martin gave a New Year's party.
4. Who did Professor Brown give a party for? She gave a party for her students.
5. Who gave a birthday party? Mrs. Adams gave a birthday party.
6. Who gave a graduation party? Professor Brown gave a graduation party.
7. Who did Dr. Martin give a party for? He gave a party for his employees.
8. Who did Mrs. Adams give a party for? She gave a party for her son.

◇ **PRACTICE 10, p. 134.**

1. forget
2. give
3. understand
4. hurt
5. spend
6. cost
7. lend
8. cut
9. hit
10. make
11. shut

◇ **PRACTICE 11, p. 134.**

1. shut
2. forgot
3. made
4. gave
5. understood
6. cut/hurt
7. cost
8. spent
9. lent/gave
10. hit/hurt
11. hurt

◇ **PRACTICE 12, p. 135.**

1. know
2. feel
3. keep
4. swim
5. throw
6. draw
7. grow
8. fall
9. win
10. blow

◇ **PRACTICE 13, p. 136.**

1. blew
2. drew
3. fell
4. felt
5. threw
6. grew
7. kept
8. swam
9. knew
10. won

◇ **PRACTICE 14, p. 136.**

1. hold
2. bend
3. shake
4. become
5. feed
6. bite
7. hide
8. fight
9. build

◇ **PRACTICE 15, p. 137.**

1. built
2. shook
3. fed
4. hid
5. bit/shook/held
6. became
7. fought
8. held
9. bent/bit

◇ **PRACTICE 16, p. 138.**

Incomplete	*Complete*
at the store	We slept.
after they left	They left.
after several minutes	Before school starts, I help the teacher.
before school starts	We ate at a restaurant.
after we finish dinner	We were at home.

◇ **PRACTICE 17, p. 139.**

1. 1, 2
   After my computer crashed, I lost my information. OR
   I lost my information after my computer crashed.
2. 2, 1
   After I looked in the freezer, I closed the freezer door.
   OR
   I closed the freezer door after I looked in the freezer.
3. 1, 2
   After I stood on the scale, the nurse wrote down my weight. OR
   The nurse wrote down my weight after I stood on the scale.
4. 2, 1
   After I put on my exercise clothes, I exercised. OR
   I exercised after I put on my exercise clothes.
5. 2, 1
   After the sun came out, the snow began to melt. OR
   The snow began to melt after the sun came out.

◇ **PRACTICE 18, p. 139.**

1. 1, 2
   a, d
2. 2, 1
   b, c
3. 2, 1
   a, d
4. 1, 2
   b, c

◇ **PRACTICE 19, p. 140.**

1. a. When you called,
   b. When did you call?
2. a. When did the movie start?
   b. When the movie started,
3. a. When you were in high school,
   b. When were you in high school?
4. a. When it snowed,
   b. When did it snow?
5. a. When was Dave sick?
   b. When Dave was sick,

◇ **PRACTICE 20, p. 141.**

1. When was the Smith's party?
2. When the Browns came, I met them at the airport.
3. When did you hear the good news?
4. When Mr. King died, we felt sad.
5. When were you here?
6. When did we meet?
7. When you arrived, we were happy to see you.
8. When Kevin was absent, the class had a test.
9. When the movie ended, everyone clapped.
10. When was Mrs. Allen a teacher?

◇ **PRACTICE 21, p. 141.**
Answers will vary in "b" sentences.
1. a. When did it rain?
   b. When it rained, I went inside.
2. a. When did you get sick?
   b. When you got sick, I worried about you.
3. a. When did the movie begin?
   b. When the movie began, we were outside the theater.
4. a. When did they visit?
   b. When they visited, we went to the zoo.

◇ **PRACTICE 22, p. 142.**
1. was studying
2. were studying
3. was studying
4. was studying
5. were studying
6. were studying
7. were not studying
8. were not studying
9. was not studying
10. were not studying
11. were not studying
12. was not studying

◇ **PRACTICE 23, p. 142.**
1. am sitting
2. was sitting
3. are sitting
4. were sitting
5. is sitting
6. was sitting
7. are sitting
8. were sitting
9. is sitting
10. was sitting
11. are sitting
12. were sitting

◇ **PRACTICE 24, p. 143.**
1. a. We felt an earthquake while we were sitting in our living room last night,
   b. While we were sitting in our living room, we felt an earthquake.
2. a. While I was talking to the teacher yesterday, another student interrupted me.
   b. Another student interrupted me while I was talking to the teacher yesterday.
3. a. While I was planting flowers in the garden, my dog began to bark at a squirrel.
   b. My dog began to bark at a squirrel while I was planting flowers in the garden.
4. a. A police officer stopped another driver for speeding while we were driving to work.
   b. While we were driving to work, a police officer stopped another driver for speeding.
5. a. While I was walking in the forest, a dead tree fell over.
   b. A dead tree fell over while I was walking in the forest.

◇ **PRACTICE 25, p. 144.**
1. was driving
2. rang
3. didn't answer
4. wanted
5. noticed
6. was slowing
7. drove
8. saw

◇ **PRACTICE 26, p. 144.**
1. were
2. were sitting
3. came
4. screamed
5. did your cousin do
6. yelled
7. Did your husband do
8. ran
9. was running
10. ran
11. began

◇ **PRACTICE 27, p. 144.**
1. was sleeping . . . got
2. called . . . was taking
3. was eating . . . remembered
4. started . . . became
5. was driving . . . saw
6. was exercising . . . came

◇ **PRACTICE 28, p. 145.**
1. Where did Ann go?
2. When did Ann go to the zoo?
3. Who went to the zoo yesterday?
4. Who did you see?
5. Where did you see Ali?
6. When did you see Ali at the zoo?
7. Why did you go to the zoo yesterday?
8. Who called?
9. When did they call?
10. Who did you talk to?
11. Where were you yesterday afternoon?
12. What does "ancient" mean?
13. Where are you living?
14. What is the teacher talking about?
15. What does Annie have in her pocket?

◇ **PRACTICE 29, p. 146.**
Sample answers:
1. When did you get up this morning?
2. Where do you live?
3. When did you arrive?
4. What does "terrific" mean?
5. What time does the movie start?
6. What did you buy?
7. What are you making for dinner?
8. Did you get home early yesterday/
9. Why did you work late?
10. What are you studying?
11. Did you do well on your test?
12. What are you doing?
13. Where was the party?
14. Why didn't you go to the party?
15. When were you at the library?

◇ **PRACTICE 30, p. 146.**
1. He said they were too noisy.
2. She caught a cold yesterday.
3. She found it on the teacher's desk.
4. Someone stole his wallet.
5. He ate too much for lunch.
6. It sold in three days.
7. It tore when she played outside.
8. She hung up after midnight.
9. Sam bent over and picked it up for her.
10. I caught a taxi.
11. Several students came to class without their homework.
12. I grew up there.

1. threw   7. cost
2. broke   8. knew
3. told   9. met
4. spent   10. fell
5. made   11. lost
6. wore   12. stole

◇ PRACTICE 32, p. 148.

1. began   6. shook
2. sang   7. built
3. flew   8. put
4. left   9. fought
5. won   10. fed

◇ PRACTICE 33, p. 149.

PART I.
1. was   6. heard
2. went   7. got
3. overslept   8. ran
4. didn't ring 9. was
5. woke   10. was

PART II.
11. went   17. went
12. had   18. got
13. dropped   19. paid
14. broke   20. sat
15. dropped   21. ate
16. looked   22. drank

PART III.
23. went   28. talked
24. sat   29. relaxed
25. saw   30. stood
26. called   31. stepped
27. joined   32. broke

PART IV.
33. drove   37. paid
34. went   38. left
35. took   39. took
36. put   40. helped

PART V.
41. got   47. waited
42. looked   48. came
43. rang   49. got
44. thought   50. ate
45. wasn't   51. went
46. sat   52. slept

Chapter 10: EXPRESSING FUTURE TIME, PART 1

◇ PRACTICE 1, p. 152.

1. am going to be   6. are going to be
2. are going to be   7. is going to be
3. is going to be   8. is going to be
4. are going to be   9. are going to be
5. are going to be

◇ PRACTICE 2, p. 152.

1. A: Are you going to be
   B: am going to be
2. A: is your roommate going to go
   B: is going to stay
   B: is going to look
3. A: are you going to do
   B: am going to study
   A: am going to relax
4. A: Are Ed and Nancy going to join
   B: are going to meet

◇ PRACTICE 3, p. 153.

1. going to go back to bed.
2. am going to eat a big lunch.
3. am going to take some medicine.
4. am going to call the neighbors.
5. is going to do a search on the Internet.
6. are going to look for a bigger place.
7. is going to check the lost-and-found.
8. am going to take it back.

◇ PRACTICE 4, p. 154.

He **is going to wake up** at 9:00. He **is going to watch** sports on TV for a while. Then he **is going to go** to a café for breakfast. After breakfast, he **is going to call up** his friends. They **are going to make** plans for the weekend. He **is going to rent** a DVD for the afternoon. Before dinner, he **is going to check** his e-mail. For dinner, he **is going to pick up** fast food. Later he **is going to go** to the gym, but not for exercise. He **is going to sit** next to the exercise machines with his best friend. They **are going to talk** about their busy day.

◇ PRACTICE 5, p. 154.

Sample answers:
1. I am going to get a drink of water.
2. I am going to drink tea with honey.
3. I am going to call the dentist.
4. I am going to get ready quickly.
5. I am going to take a hot bath.
6. I am going to call the police.

◇ PRACTICE 6, p. 155.

Negative	Question
1. I am not going to eat.	Am I going to eat?
2. You are not going to eat.	Are you going to eat?
3. He is not going to eat.	Is he going to eat?
4. She is not going to eat.	Is she going to eat?
5. We are not going to eat.	Are we going to eat?
6. They are not going to eat.	Are they going to eat?
7. My friend is not going to eat.	Is my friend going to eat?
8. The students are not going to eat.	Are the students going to eat?

PRACTICE 7, p. 155.

1. A: are you going to do
   B: are going to go
   A: Are you going to stay
   B: are going to come
2. A: is Sally going to work
   B: is not going to work . . . is going to take
3. A: Are the students going to have
   B: are going to have
4. A: Are Joan and Bob going to move
   B: is going to start
   A: Are they going to look for
   B: they are not going to look for . . . are going to rent

PRACTICE 8, p. 156.

1. The Johnsons are taking a camping trip across Canada this summer.
2. They are taking their teenage grandchildren with them.
3. They are staying in parks and campgrounds.
4. They are leaving from Vancouver in June.
5. They are arriving in Montreal in August.
6. Mr. and Mrs. Johnson are driving back home alone.
7. Their grandchildren are flying home because they don't want to miss the beginning of school.
8. Their parents are meeting them at the airport.

PRACTICE 9, p. 157.

1. P	4. F	7. F
2. F	5. F	8. P
3. F	6. P	9. P

PRACTICE 10, p. 157.

1. last	8. tomorrow
2. ago	9. in
3. ago	10. yesterday
4. last	11. last
5. next	12. tomorrow
6. in	13. ago
7. yesterday	14. next

PRACTICE 11, p. 158.

Checked sentences and rewrites:
2. a couple of hours
6. a couple of years
9. a couple of weeks

PRACTICE 12, p. 158.

Checked sentences and rewrites:
1. a few minutes
3. a few hours
4. a few days
6. a few years

PRACTICE 13, p. 158.

1. a. I am going to leave in a few days.
   b. I left a few days ago.
2. a. Susie is going to marry Paul in a couple of months.
   b. Susie married Paul a couple of months ago.
3. a. Dr. Nelson retired a few years ago.
   b. Dr. Nelson is going to retire in a few years.

4. a. Jack began a new job a couple of days ago.
   b. Jack is going to begin a new job in a couple of days.

PRACTICE 14, p. 159.

1. future		7. present
2. past		8. past
3. present		9. future
4. past		10. past
5. future		11. future
6. present		

PRACTICE 15, p. 160.

1. a. She woke up late.
   b. She looked at her alarm clock. OR She missed her history class.
2. a. She is going to sit at the kitchen table.
   b. She is going to think about a solution.
3. She is sitting in her kitchen.

PRACTICE 16, p. 160.

1. a
2. b
3. a

PRACTICE 17, p. 160.

1. will be	6. will be
2. will be	7. will be
3. will be	8. will be
4. will be	9. will be
5. will be	10. will be

PRACTICE 18, p. 161.

Free response.

PRACTICE 19, p. 161.

Free response.

PRACTICE 20. P. 162.

1. Class will finish a few minutes early today.
2. I will pick you up after school.
3. Hurry or we won't be on time for the movie.
4. Your brother and sister will help you with your science project.
5. The bus won't be on time today.
6. You will cut yourself with that sharp knife.
7. Carlos and Olivia will graduate from nursing school next year.

PRACTICE 21, p. 162.

	be going to + *go*	*will* + *go*
1.	am going to go	will go
2.	are going to go	will go
3.	are going to go	will go
4.	is going to go	will go
5.	are going to go	will go
6.	is not going to go	won't go
7.	am not going to go	won't go
8.	are not going to go	won't go
9.	Is she going to go?	Will she go?
10.	Are they going to go?	Will they go?
11.	Are you going to go?	Will you go?

◇ PRACTICE 22, p. 163.

1. Will you live to be 100 years old?
2. Will your friends live to be 100 years old?
3. Will your children live to be 100 years old?
4. Will we live on another planet?
5. Will my friends live on another planet?
6. Will some people live underwater?
7. Will I live underwater?
8. Will countries find a solution for poverty?

◇ PRACTICE 23, p. 164.

1. Will he change his behavior? Yes, he will.
2. Will he do his homework every night? Yes, he will.
3. Will he forget to bring his homework to school? No, he won't.
4. Will he go to parties on weekends? No, he won't.
5. Will he eat junk food? No, he won't.
6. Will he eat healthy food? Yes, he will.
7. Will he exercise often? Yes, he will.
8. Will he be a better student? Yes, he will.

◇ PRACTICE 24, p. 165.

1. Do you need help now?
2. Are you going to need help tomorrow? OR Will you need help tomorrow?
3. Did you need help yesterday?
4. Did Eva need help yesterday?
5. Is Eva going to need help tomorrow? OR Will Eva need help tomorrow?
6. Does Eva need help now?
7. Do the students need help now?
8. Are the students going to need help tomorrow? OR Will the students need help tomorrow?
9. Did the students need help yesterday?

◇ PRACTICE 25, p. 165.

1. is eating
2. eats
3. eats
4. ate
5. cooked
6. was . . . loved
7. dropped . . . was . . . didn't burn
8. is going to have / will have
9. Is she going to cook / Will she cook
10. Is she going to fix / Will she fix
11. isn't going to prepare / won't prepare
12. is going to surprise / will surprise

◇ PRACTICE 26, p. 166.

1. Are you sick now?
2. Are you going to be sick tomorrow? OR Will you be sick tomorrow?
3. Were you sick yesterday?
4. Was Steve sick yesterday?
5. Is Steve going to be sick tomorrow? OR Will Steve be sick tomorrow?
6. Is Steve sick now?
7. Are the children sick now?
8. Are the children going to be sick tomorrow? OR Will be children be sick tomorrow?
9. Were the children sick yesterday?

◇ PRACTICE 27, p. 127.

1. am . . . am . . . am going to be / will be . . . was . . . am going to be / will be
2. A: were you . . . Were you
   B: wasn't . . . was
   A: was . . . were you
   B: were
   A: was
3. A: Is a dolphin
   B: isn't . . . is
   A: Are they
   B: aren't . . . are
   A: Are you going to be / Will you be
   B: am going to be / will be

◇ PRACTICE 28, p. 167.

1. Do
2. Do
3. Are
4. Do
5. Are
6. Do
7. Are
8. Are
9. Do

◇ PRACTICE 29, p. 168.

1. Did
2. Did
3. Were
4. Were
5. Did
6. Did
7. Did
8. Were

◇ PRACTICE 30, p. 168.

	Every day/now	Yesterday	Tomorrow
1.	drink / am drinking	drank	am going to drink / will drink
2.	work / are working	worked	am going to work / will work
3.	is / is	was	is going to be / will be
4.	help / are helping	helped	are going to help / will help
5.	doesn't come / isn't coming	didn't come	isn't going to come / won't come
6.	doesn't do / isn't doing	didn't do	isn't going to do / won't do
7.	Do they exercise / Are they exercising	Did they exercise	Are they going to exercise / Will they exercise
8.	Is he / Is he	Was he	Is he going to be / Will he be
9.	isn't / isn't	wasn't	isn't going to be / won't be

◇ PRACTICE 31, p. 169.

1. A: lost
   A: think . . . left
2. A: are you going to wear / will you wear / are you wearing
   B: am going to wear / will wear / am wearing . . . is going to be / will be / is
3. A: Did she tell . . . did she tell
   B: told
4. am making . . . is getting
5. A: did you go
   B: went . . . saw . . . talked . . . met . . . like

6. A: Are you going to study / Will you study / Are you
     studying
   B: don't have
   B: gave . . . is giving
7. A: Did you do
   B: was . . . went . . . slept
8. A: said
   B: didn't understand
9. A: is Cathy
   B: is meeting
10. had . . . ran . . . slammed . . . missed
11. played . . . caught . . . dropped
12. A: Did you send
    B: forgot

Chapter 11: EXPRESSING FUTURE TIME, PART 2

◇ PRACTICE 1, p. 171.
1. unsure   6. unsure
2. sure   7. sure
3. sure   8. unsure
4. unsure   9. unsure
5. unsure   10. sure

◇ PRACTICE 2, p. 171.
Free response.

◇ PRACTICE 3, p. 172.
1. a. It may be sunny tomorrow.
   b. Maybe it will be sunny tomorrow.
2. a. You might need to see a doctor soon.
   b. Maybe you will need to see a doctor soon.
3. a. We might play soccer after school.
   b. We may play soccer after school.
4. a. Maybe our class will go to a movie together.
   b. Our class may go to a movie together.

◇ PRACTICE 4, p. 172.
1. b   3. a, b   5. b
2. b   4. a   6. a, b

◇ PRACTICE 5, p. 172.
1. I may study.   I might study.
2. They may study.   They might study.
3. She might not study.   Maybe she won't study.
4. We might need help.   Maybe we will need help.
5. I might not need help.   Maybe I won't need help.
6. He may understand.   Maybe he will understand.
7. You may understand.   Maybe you will understand.
8. They may not   Maybe they won't
   understand.   understand.

◇ PRACTICE 6, p. 173.
1. It will snow tomorrow.
2. It may/might snow next week OR Maybe it will snow
   next week.
3. We may/might go ice-skating. OR Maybe we will go
   ice-skating.
4. The children will play in the snow.
5. The snow won't melt for several days.

◇ PRACTICE 7, p. 173.
1. a, c, d   3. a, b, c
2. a, b, d   4. b, d

◇ PRACTICE 8, p. 174.
1. 1, 2
   a. After I boil the water, I am going to put in the rice.
   b. Before I put in the rice, I am going to boil the water.
2. 2, 1
   a. After I check my answers one time, I am going to
      turn in my homework.
   b. Before I turn in my homework, I am going to check
      my answers one time.
3. 2, 1
   a. After I clear off the table, I am going to wash the
      dishes.
   b. Before I wash the dishes, I am going to clear off the
      table.
4. 1, 2
   a. After I put on warm clothes, I am going to go out in
      the snow.
   b. Before I go out in the snow, I am going to put on
      warm clothes.
5. 2, 1
   a. After I go to the departure gate, I am going to go
      board the airplane.
   b. Before I board the airplane, I am going to go to the
      departure gate.

◇ PRACTICE 9, p. 175.
1. he gets up, he is going to/will make breakfast.
2. he goes to school, he is going to/will eat breakfast.
3. he gets to school, he is going to go/will go to his
   classroom.
4. he has lunch in the cafeteria, he is going to/will talk to
   his friends.
5. he cooks dinner for his roommates, he is going to pick
   up/will pick up food for dinner.
6. he goes to bed, he is going to do/will do his homework.
7. he falls asleep, he is going to have/will have good
   dreams.

◇ PRACTICE 10, p. 175.
1. fix . . . am going to get/will get
2. have . . . am going to go/will go
3. see . . . are going to make/will make
4. takes . . . is going to practice/will practice
5. is going to feel/will feel . . . takes
6. gets . . . is going to be/will be

◇ PRACTICE 11, p. 176.
1. wins . . . will attend
2. goes . . . is going to study
3. enjoys . . . will take
4. will apply . . . does
5. attends . . . is going to major in
6. completes . . . is going to work

◇ PRACTICE 12, p. 176.
1. is . . . is going to work/will work
2. rains . . . am not going to work/won't work
3. gets . . . are going to be/will be
4. are going to get/will get . . . does not do
5. gets . . . is going to earn/will earn
6. doesn't get . . . is going to delay/will delay
7. feels . . . is not going to come/won't come
8. is going to call/will call . . . misses
9. needs . . . are going to help/will help
10. are going to make/will make . . . doesn't need

◇ PRACTICE 13, p. 177.
1. is going to ask/will ask
2. celebrate
3. talks
4. is going to meet/will meet
5. agree
6. is going to buy/will buy
7. says
8. is going to give/will give
9. doesn't say
10. is going to keep/will keep

◇ PRACTICE 14, p. 177.
PART I.
1. F   4. C   6. G
2. A   5. B   7. D
3. E

PART II.
1. If I drink too much coffee, I feel shaky and nervous.
2. If I cry, my eyes get red.
3. If I don't pay my electric bill, I have no electricity.
4. If the phone rings in the middle of the night, I don't answer it.
5. If I get to work late, I get home late.
6. If I have a big breakfast, I have a lot of energy.
7. If I don't do my homework, I get low grades on the tests.

◇ PRACTICE 15, p. 178.
Sample answers:
1. a. If I'm late for class, I feel nervous.
   b. I feel nervous if I'm late for class.
2. a. After I eat too much, I feel sick.
   b. I feel sick after I eat too much.
3. a. If I get a headache, I take some headache medicine.
   b. I take some headache medicine if I get a headache.
4. a. When my teacher talks too fast, I ask him/her to repeat.
   b. I ask my teacher to repeat when he/she talks too fast.

◇ PRACTICE 16, p. 179.
1. present habit   6. future
2. future   7. future
3. future   8. present habit
4. present habit   9. future
5. present habit

◇ PRACTICE 17, p. 179.
1. like . . . is
2. are going to go/will go . . . is

3. go . . . am going to meet/will meet
4. go . . . usually meet
5. am going to buy/will buy . . . go
6. is . . . gets . . . feels . . . exercises . . . exercises . . . begins
7. am . . . am not going to exercise/will not exercise
8. travel . . . bring
9. travel . . . are going to pack/will pack
10. is . . . begins
11. gets . . . is going to tell/will tell

◇ PRACTICE 18, p. 180.
1. What are they doing
2. What did they do
3. What are they going to do
4. What will they do
5. What do they do
6. What is she doing now?
7. What did you do last night?
8. What will she do?
9. What are you going to do?
10. What does he do?

◇ PRACTICE 19, p. 181.
1. What does he do?
2. What do you do?
3. What do you do?
4. What do they do?
5. What does she do?
6. What do Thomas and Joanne do?
7. What do I do?

◇ PRACTICE 20, p. 181.
1. B   4. A   7. C
2. C   5. D   8. D
3. C   6. A

Chapter 12: MODALS, PART 1: EXPRESSING ABILITY

◇ PRACTICE 1, p. 183.
1. can speak   7. can speak
2. can speak   8. can speak
3. can speak   9. can speak
4. can speak   10. can speak
5. can speak   11. can speak
6. can speak

◇ PRACTICE 2, p. 183.
1. can   3. can't   5. can
2. can't   4. can   6. can

◇ PRACTICE 3, p. 184.
Free response.

◇ PRACTICE 4, p. 184.
1. Can Mia drive a car? Yes, she can.
2. Can George and Eva play the piano? Yes, they can.
3. Can George repair a bike? No, he can't.
4. Can Paul play the piano? Yes, he can.
5. Can Mia, George, and Paul swim? Yes, they can.
6. Can Paul and Eva drive a car? No, they can't.
7.–9. *Free response.*

PRACTICE 5, p. 185.

1. Can you type? Yes, I can.
2. Can you do work processing? Yes, I can.
3. Can you speak English? No, I can't.
4. Can you lift suitcases? No, I can't.
5. Can you work weekends? Yes, I can.

PRACTICE 6, p. 185.

1. Toni knows how to make pizza.
2. Martha knows how to play chess.
3. Sonya and Thomas know how to speak Portuguese.
4. Jack doesn't know how to speak Russian.
5. My brothers don't know how to cook.
6. I don't know how to change a flat tire.
7. We don't know how to play musical instruments.
8. Do you know how to type?
9. Do your children know how to swim?
10. Does Ari know how to use a digital camera?

PRACTICE 7, p. 186.

Free response.

PRACTICE 8, p. 187.

1. They couldn't watch TV.
2. They could cook over a fire.
3. They could read books.
4. They could spend time together.
5. They couldn't use a computer.
6. They couldn't turn on the lights.

7. They couldn't use electric heat.
8. They could have heat from a woodstove.
9. They could play board games.

PRACTICE 9, p. 188.

1. couldn't
2. can't
3. Could
4. can
5. could
6. Could
7. can't

PRACTICE 10, p. 188.

Order will vary.

1. he couldn't drive a car . . .
   he can drive a car.
2. he couldn't go swimming . . .
   he can go swimming.
3. he couldn't play soccer . . .
   he can play soccer.
4. he couldn't ride a bike . . .
   he can ride a bike.

PRACTICE 11, p. 189.

1. couldn't
2. couldn't
3. could/couldn't
4. could/couldn't
5. can
6. can/can't
7. can/can't

PRACTICE 12, p. 189.

Present	Past	Future
1. I am able to run.	I was able to run.	I will be able to run.
2. You are able to draw.	You were able to draw.	You will be able to draw.
3. He is able to drive.	He was able to drive.	He will be able to drive.
4. She is able to swim.	She was able to swim.	She will be able to swim.
5. We are able to dance.	We were able to dance.	She will be able to dance.
6. They are able to type.	They were able to type.	They will be able to type.

PRACTICE 13, p. 189.

1. wasn't able to
2. wasn't able to
3. was able to/wasn't able to
4. was able to/wasn't able to
5. am able to
6. am able to/am not able to
7. am able to/am not able to

PRACTICE 14, p. 190.

1. wasn't able to speak
2. wasn't able to ask
3. weren't able to give
4. wasn't able to visit
5. wasn't able to have
6. was able to understand
7. were able to have
8. was able to learn
9. was able to visit

PRACTICE 15, p. 190.

1. b
2. a
3. b
4. c
5. c

PRACTICE 16, p. 191.

1. too
2. very
3. very
4. too
5. too
6. too
7. very
8. very

PRACTICE 17, p. 191.

1. A
2. A
3. B
4. B
5. A
6. A
7. B
8. A

PRACTICE 18, p. 192.

Free response.

PRACTICE 19, p. 192.

1. two
2. to
3. too . . . too
4. to . . . too
5. to . . . To . . . To
6. too . . . too
7. Two . . . to
8. too

PRACTICE 20, p. 192.

1. two
2. to
3. to
4. too
5. to
6. two
7. two
8. to
9. too

PRACTICE 21, p. 193.

1. at
2. at
3. at
4. in
5. in
6. at
7. at
8. in
9. in
10. in

PRACTICE 22, p. 193.

1. in . . . at
2. in *(also possible:* at)
3. in . . . at
4. at . . . in
5. in
6. at . . . at
7. in

PRACTICE 23, p. 194.

1. B
2. C
3. D
4. A
5. D
6. C
7. C
8. B

PRACTICE 24, p. 194.

1. was
2. hunted
3. took
4. listened
5. dreamed/dreamt
6. decided
7. are you leaving
8. are you going/will you go
9. am going
10. am going
11. do you want
12. to go
13. want
14. to experience
15. need
16. to learn
17. can learn
18. stay
19. stay
20. can't stay
21. is
22. will have
23. get
24. will face
25. may never see
26. will try
27. Are you having/ Do you have
28. can I cross
29. don't know
30. can't cross
31. won't be
32. will help
33. will give
34. can jump
35. will also give
36. don't lose
37. will reach
38. are you lying
39. Are you
40. can't see
41. drank
42. am
43. will die
44. can't find
45. gave
46. can I give
47. will give
48. can see
49. can't see
50. will you find
51. Jump
52. will carry
53. can't go
54. will I do
55. have
56. Keep
57. will find
58. can't see
59. can hear
60. can't help
61. am dying
62. are you dying
63. lost
64. can't find
65. am starving/will starve
66. can help
67. will give
68. can smell
69. can I help
70. am trying
71. need
72. to go
73. Come
74. will put
75. (will) take
76. couldn't see
77. couldn't smell
78. lost
79. heard
80. help
81. Don't cry
82. aren't
83. never lost
84. Jump
85. Use
86. am flying/can fly

Chapter 13: MODALS, PART 2: ADVICE, NECESSITY, REQUESTS, SUGGESTIONS

PRACTICE 1, p. 199.

1. should study
2. should study
3. should study
4. should study
5. should study
6. should study
7. should study
8. should study
9. should study

PRACTICE 2, p. 199.

1. should
2. should
3. shouldn't
4. shouldn't
5. should
6. should
7. shouldn't

PRACTICE 3, p. 200.

1. She should do her homework.
2. She shouldn't copy her roommate's homework.
3. She should study for her tests.
4. She shouldn't stay up late.
5. She shouldn't daydream in class.
6. She shouldn't be absent from class a lot.
7. She should take notes during lectures.
8. She should take her books to school.

PRACTICE 4, p. 200.

Sample answers:
1. should clean her room. (Note: In this case, *room* means "bedroom.")
2. should ask them to turn down the music.
3. shouldn't dance for a while.
4. should see a dentist.
5. should save his money.
6. should get visas.

PRACTICE 5, p. 201.

1. have to leave
2. have to leave
3. have to leave
4. have to leave
5. has to leave
6. has to leave
7. don't have to leave
8. don't have to leave
9. doesn't have to leave
10. don't have to leave

PRACTICE 6, p. 201.

1. has to
2. doesn't have to
3. has to
4. doesn't have to
5. doesn't have to
6. has to
7. has to

PRACTICE 7, p. 202.

1. have to
2. don't have to
3. has to
4. have to
5. don't have to
6. have to
7. doesn't have to
8. have to
9. has to
10. doesn't have to

PRACTICE 8, p. 202.

1. had to
2. had to
3. didn't have to
4. had to
5. didn't have to
6. had to
7. didn't have to
8. had to

Free response.

◇ PRACTICE 10, p. 203.

Free response.

◇ PRACTICE 11, p. 204.
1. must
2. must
3. must not
4. must
5. must not
6. must not

◇ PRACTICE 12, p. 204.
1. must
2. must not
3. must
4. must not
5. must
6. must

◇ PRACTICE 13, p. 205.
1. should
2. must
3. must
4. should
5. must
6. should
7. must
8. should
9. should

◇ PRACTICE 14, p. 206.
1. May I/Could I/Can I have some hot coffee, please?
2. May I/Could I/Can I look at your dictionary for a minute, please?
3. May I/Could I/Can I sharpen my pencil, please?
4. May I/Could I/Can I borrow your cell phone, please?
5. May I/Could I/Can I get a new library card, please?

◇ PRACTICE 15, p. 206.
(Note: "please" can come in the middle or at the end of a question.)
1. Could/Would you please repeat the question?
2. Could/Would you please clean your bedroom?
3. Could/Would you give me some money for a movie, please?
4. Could/Would you turn down the TV, please?
5. Could/Would you bring me some fresh cream, please?
6. Could/Would you please take our picture?

◇ PRACTICE 16, p. 206.
1. Professor: <u>Come</u> in.
2. Teacher: <u>Read</u> pages . . . and <u>answer</u> the questions . . .
3. Heidi: Please <u>close</u> the window, Mike . . . please <u>hand</u> me . . .
   Mike: <u>Take</u> care of yourself . . . <u>Take</u> good care
   Heidi: <u>Don't worry</u>.

◇ PRACTICE 17, p. 207.
1. Put oil in a pan.
2. Heat the oil.
3. Put the popcorn in a pan.
4. Cover the pan with a lid.
5. Shake the pan.
6. Stop shaking the pan when the popcorn stops popping.
7. Pour the popcorn into a bowl.
8. Pour melted butter over the popcorn.
9. Salt the popcorn.
10. Enjoy your snack!

◇ PRACTICE 18, p. 208.
1. Sit
2. Don't chew
3. Don't talk
4. Do
5. Don't copy *(also possible:* Don't do*)*
6. Work
7. Answer

◇ PRACTICE 19, p. 208.
1. Show
2. Don't bring
3. Follow
4. Turn off
5. Don't play
6. Use
7. Talk
8. Ask
9. Don't download

◇ PRACTICE 20, p. 209.
1. to
2. Ø
3. Ø
4. to
5. Ø
6. Ø
7. to
8. Ø
9. to
10. Ø

◇ PRACTICE 21, p. 209.
1. b
2. a
3. b
4. c
5. c
6. c
7. a
8. b

◇ PRACTICE 22, p. 210.
Sample answers:
1. Let's go to the park.
2. Let's relax tonight.
3. Let's have a party for her.
4. Let's eat.
5. Let's have dinner there.

◇ PRACTICE 23, p. 210.
1. B
2. C
3. C
4. A
5. B
6. A
7. C
8. B
9. C
10. A

Chapter 14: NOUNS AND MODIFIERS

◇ PRACTICE 1, p. 212.

Adjectives	Nouns
tall	clothes
pretty	pens
sad	boat
hot	store
true	horse
happy	truth

◇ PRACTICE 2, p. 212.

Sample answers:

interesting song	happy person
chicken soup	nutritious food
grammar book	boring story
English language	wonderful news

◇ PRACTICE 3, p. 213.

1. adjective
2. noun
3. noun
4. adjective
5. adjective
6. noun
7. noun
8. adjective

◇ PRACTICE 4, p. 213.

Sample answers:
1. heavy traffic . . . traffic sign
2. difficult grammar . . . grammar book
3. big apartment . . . apartment building
4. old newspaper . . . newspaper article
5. loud music . . . music teacher

◇ PRACTICE 5, p. 214.

1. dog house.
2. magazine article.
3. business card.
4. dentist appointment.
5. chicken salad.
6. house key.
7. computer printer.
8. milk carton.
9. clothes store.
10. shower curtain.

◇ PRACTICE 6, p. 214.

1. birthday present
   happy birthday
   birthday cake
2. messy kitchen
   kitchen cabinets
   kitchen counter
3. city bus
   bus schedule
   bus route
4. airplane noise
   airplane movie
   airplane ticket
5. apartment manager
   one-bedroom apartment
   apartment building
6. phone number
   cell phone
   phone call
7. hospital patient
   sick patient
   patient information

◇ PRACTICE 7, p. 214.

1. small 100-year-old house
2. spicy Mexican food
3. kind young man
4. dirty brown glass
5. lovely tall rose bush
6. interesting small old paintings
7. important new foreign film
8. little yellow flowers
9. tall middle-aged woman
10. an antique Chinese wooden cabinet

◇ PRACTICE 8, p. 216.

1. A
2. B
3. B
4. B
5. A
6. A
7. B
8. A

◇ PRACTICE 9, p. 217.

1. a
2. c
3. a or b
4. a

◇ PRACTICE 10, p. 217.

1. 95%
2. 90%
3. 100%
4. 60%
5. 50%
6. 75%
7. 30%
8. 88%
9. 100%
10. 97%

◇ PRACTICE 11, p. 217.

1. is
2. are
3. is
4. are
5. is
6. are
7. are
8. is
9. are
10. is
11. are
12. is
13. is
14. are
15. is
16. are

◇ PRACTICE 12, p. 218.

1. friends
2. classes
3. teachers
4. meals
5. shoes
6. friends
7. words
8. children
9. movies
10. problems

◇ PRACTICE 13, p. 218.

1. is/are
2. is
3. fit/fits
4. fits
5. has/have
6. has
7. is/are
8. teaches
9. take/takes
10. is
11. looks
12. seems

◇ PRACTICE 14, p. 219.

1. One of the test questions has a mistake.
2. None of the questions is/are easy.
3. One of my cousins works with me.
4. None of the jewelry is very valuable.
5. None of the rings is/are very expensive.
6. One of my teachers has several grandchildren.

◇ PRACTICE 15, p. 220.

1. One of
2. None of
3. Almost all of
4. None of
5. All of
6. One of
7. None of
8. Some of
9. None of
10. Almost all of

◇ PRACTICE 16, p. 220.

1. is
2. are
3. is
4. is
5. is
6. are
7. is
8. are
9. is/are
10. are

◇ PRACTICE 17, p. 221.

1. a. anyone
   b. no one
2. a. anything
   b. nothing
3. a. nothing
   b. anything
4. a. anyone
   b. no one

◇ PRACTICE 18, p. 221.

1. anything
2. nothing
3. anyone. No one
4. nothing
5. nothing
6. anyone
7. anything
8. nothing
9. anyone
10. no one

◇ PRACTICE 19, p. 221.

	Statement	Negative
1.	something	anything
2.	someone	anyone
3.	something	anything
4.	someone	anyone
5.	someone	anyone
6.	something	anything
7.	someone	anyone
8.	something	anything

◇ PRACTICE 20, p. 222.

1. anything
2. anyone
3. something
4. someone
5. a. something
   b. anything
6. a. someone
   b. anyone

◇ PRACTICE 21, p. 222.

1. A: something
   B: anything
2. A: something/anything
   B: anything
3. A: someone . . . someone
   B: anyone
4. A: anyone
   B: Someone
5. A: something/anything
   B: anything
6. A: someone/something
   B: anyone/anything
   A: anyone or anything OR anything or anyone

◇ PRACTICE 22, p. 223.

1. B   4. B   7. A
2. A   5. A   8. B
3. B   6. B

◇ PRACTICE 23, p. 223.

1. B   5. A   9. A
2. A   6. B   10. A
3. B   7. A
4. A   8. B

◇ PRACTICE 24, p. 224.

1. **Every teacher** is on time.
2. Every **student** is on time too.
3. *(correct)*
4. Everything in the sink **is** dirty.
5. Where **do** all of your friends live?
6. *(correct)*
7. Everybody in my family **likes** dessert after dinner.
8. **Does** everyone in your family **like** dessert?
9. *(correct)*
10. **Were** all of the people at the wedding your friends?
11. Everyone **is** friendly.
12. *(correct)*

◇ PRACTICE 25, p. 224.

Checked sentences and linking verbs:
1. smells
2. sound
5. taste

6. smell
7. look [Note: In item 8, *look for* means "search." It is not a linking verb.]
9. felt
10. tastes

◇ PRACTICE 26, p. 225.

Sample answers:
1. interesting   5. terrible
2. tired   6. awful
3. wonderful   7. fun
4. great   8. bad

◇ PRACTICE 27, p. 225.

1. quietly   8. carefully
2. clearly   9. quickly
3. neatly   10. slowly
4. correctly   11. late
5. hard   12. honestly
6. well   13. fast
7. early   14. easily

◇ PRACTICE 28, p. 226.

1. clearly   6. hard
2. easily   7. well
3. late   8. honestly*
4. safely   9. softly
5. fast   10. carelessly*

◇ PRACTICE 29, p. 226.

1. nervous . . . nervously . . . nervously
2. beautifully . . . beautiful . . . beautiful
3. good . . . well
4. good . . . good
5. interesting . . . interesting
6. bad . . . bad
7. fast . . . fast

◇ PRACTICE 30, p. 227.

1. clearly . . . clear
2. correctly . . . correct
3. late . . . late
4. beautiful . . . beautifully
5. honest . . . honestly
6. beautiful . . . beautiful
7. good . . . good
8. easily . . . easy
9. well . . . good
10. quickly . . . quick
11. sweet . . . sweet
12. careless . . . carelessly

◇ PRACTICE 31, p. 228.

1. slow   7. fluent . . . fluently
2. slowly   8. neat
3. hard   9. carefully
4. hard   10. good
5. clear   11. well
6. early

---

*Note: Some adverbs can come before verbs.

◇ PRACTICE 32, p. 229.

1. | My wallet | is | in | my pocket. |
       subject   *be*   *prep.*   *object of prep.*

2. | A kangaroo | is | an animal. |
       subject   *be*   *noun complement*

3. | Restaurants | serve | food. |
       subject   *verb*   *object*

4. | Jason | works | in | an office. |
       subject   *verb*   *prep.*   *object of prep.*

5. | Karen | held | the baby | in | her arms. |
       subject   *verb*   *object*   *prep.*   *object of prep.*

6. | Korea | is | in | Asia. |
       subject   *be*   *prep.*   *object of prep.*

7. | Korea | is | a peninsula. |
       subject   *be*   *noun complement*

8. | Monkeys | eat | fruit. |
       subject   *verb*   *object*

9. | Children | play | with | toys. |
       subject   *verb*   *prep.*   *object of prep.*

10. | Jack | tied | a string | around | the package. |
       subject   *verb*   *object*   *prep.*   *object of prep.*

◇ PRACTICE 33, p. 230.

1. apples, bananas; b
2. apples, bananas, oranges; b
3. Jack, Olga; a
4. apples, bananas; b
5. Jack, Olga; c
6. Swimming, soccer; a
7. books, magazines; d
8. Cars, trains, trucks; a
9. planes, trains; c
10. trunk, branches, leaves, roots; b

◇ PRACTICE 34, p. 231.

1. Ants, bees, and mosquitoes are insects.
2. *(no change)*
3. Bears, tigers, and elephants are animals.
4. *(no change)*
5. I bought some rice, fruit, and vegetables at the market.
6. *(no change)*
7. The three countries in North America are Canada, the United States, and Mexico.
8. *(no change)*
9. *(no change)*
10. Shelley had some soup, a salad, and a sandwich for lunch.
11. My favorite things in life are sunny days, music, good friends, and books.
12. What do birds, butterflies, and airplanes have in common?

◇ PRACTICE 35, p. 232.

1. a   5. c   9. c
2. b   6. d   10. c
3. b   7. a   11. a
4. c   8. d   12. a

Chapter 15: POSSESSIVES

◇ PRACTICE 1, p. 234.

1. more than one   5. one
2. one   6. one
3. more than one   7. more than one
4. more than one

◇ PRACTICE 2, p. 234.

1. dog . . . Jim
2. car . . . Bill
3. desk . . . the teacher
4. schedules . . . the students
5. truck . . . my parents
6. offices . . . the professors

◇ PRACTICE 3, p. 235.

1. Ben's   5. Smith's
2. Dan's   6. pets'
3. teacher's   7. neighbors'
4. sister's   8. mother's

◇ PRACTICE 4, p. 235.

1. Tom's   5. Ø
2. Ø   6. Ø
3. Ø   7. Olga's
4. Tom's

◇ PRACTICE 5, p. 236.

1. John's   5. Marie's
2. Jane's   6. Belle's
3. Mike's   7. John's
4. Ruff's   8. Jane's

◇ PRACTICE 6, p. 236.

1. is   5. possessive
2. possessive   6. is
3. is   7. is
4. is   8. possessive

◇ PRACTICE 7, p. 237.

1. more than one   6. one
2. one   7. more than one
3. more than one   8. more than one
4. more than one   9. one
5. one

◇ PRACTICE 8, p. 237.

1. boy's truck
2. boys' trucks
3. girls' bikes
4. girl's bike
5. children's toys
6. students' books
7. woman's book
8. women's books
9. people's ideas
10. person's ideas
11. men's coats

◇ PRACTICE 9, p. 238.

1. The **children's** school is down the street.
2. Several **students'** parents help at school
3. I have one brother. I like my brother's **friends**.
4. *(correct)*
5. *(correct)*
6. I like hearing other **people's** opinions.
7. **Women's** opinions are frequently different from men's opinions.
8. Do you and your **husband** agree very often?

◇ PRACTICE 10, p. 238.

1. his	5. yours	9. his
2. hers	6. theirs	10. their
3. ours	7. her	11. your
4. mine	8. my	12. our

◇ PRACTICE 11, p. 238.

1. A
2. A [Note: B cannot be used for short answers with *be*. You need to say "Mr. Smith **is**."]
3. A
4. B
5. A
6. B
7. B

◇ PRACTICE 12, p. 239.

1. Whose book is this?
2. Whose glasses are these?
3. Whose toy is this?
4. Whose keys are these?
5. Whose shoes are these?
6. Whose shirt is this?
7. Whose cell phone is this?
8. Whose pens are these?

◇ PRACTICE 13, p. 239.

1. Who's		6. Whose
2. Whose		7. Whose
3. Who's		8. Who's
4. Who's		9. Who's
5. Whose		10. Whose

◇ PRACTICE 14, p. 240.

1. Whose pen is that?
2. Whose children are those?
3. Who is next?
4. Whose shoes are on the floor?
5. Who is absent today?
6. Whose dictionary is this?

◇ PRACTICE 15, p. 240.

1. B	4. A	7. A
2. D	5. D	8. D
3. B	6. C	

◇ PRACTICE 16, p. 241.

1. A: your
   B: It's . . . yours
2. B: mine
   C: hers
   D: his
3. A: it's
   B: Ours . . . Our . . . your
   A: Her . . . us
4. A: its
   B: It's
5. B: them
   A: them . . . their . . . their
   B: yours

◇ PRACTICE 17, p. 242.

1. A: yours
   B: mine . . . her
2. A: them
   B: her
   A: He . . . His . . . him
3. B: theirs . . . him
   A: her
4. A: yours
   B: mine . . . my
   B: them . . . yours
5. A: We . . . our
   B: you
   A: My
   B: Our
   A: Ours

◇ PRACTICE 18, p. 243.

1. That's Ann's
2. *(no change)*
3. Jim's
4. Jim's
5. He's
6. I'm
7. Tony's
8. Tony's
9. Who's
10. She's Bob's
11. *(no change)*
12. *(no change)*
13. It's Gina's
14. Where's
15. won't . . . doesn't
16. **It's** also famous . . . [Note: The first two "Its" are possessive and have no apostrophes.]

◇ PRACTICE 19, p. 244.

1. Yoko's
2. Yoko's
3. He's
4. Pablo's
5. You're
6. I'm . . . Lee's
7. Mary's . . . Anita's
8. Mary's . . . Anita's
9. That's
10. What's . . . What's . . . Who's . . . Where's
11. I'm . . . It's a grammar . . . It's on my . . . It's open
12. There's . . . It's black . . . It's sitting
13. It's a magnificent . . . It's an endangered

◇ PRACTICE 20, p. 245.

Dear Heidi,

(1)   Everything is going fine. I like **my** new apartment very much. **It's** large
(2) and comfortable. I like **my** roommate too. **His** name is Alberto. You will meet
(3) **him** when **you** visit **me** next month. **He's** from Colombia. **He's** studying English
(4) too. **We're** classmates. We were classmates last semester too. We share the rent
(5) and the utility bills, but **we** don't share the telephone bill. He pays for **his** calls
(6) and **I** pay for **mine**. **His** telephone bill is very high because he has a girlfriend
(7) in Colombia. He calls **her** often. Sometimes **she** calls **him**. **They** talk on the
(8) phone a lot.
(9)   **Our** neighbors are Mr. and Mrs. Black. **They're** very nice. We talk to **them**
(10) often. **Our** apartment is next to **theirs**. **They** have a three-year-old daughter.
(11) **She's** really cute. **Her** name is Joy. **They** also have a cat. **It's** black and white.
(12) **Its** eyes are yellow. **Its** name is Whiskers. **It's** a friendly cat. Sometimes **their**
(13) cat leaves a dead mouse outside **our** door.
(14)   **I'm** looking forward to **your** visit.

Love, Carl

Chapter 16: MAKING COMPARISONS

◇ PRACTICE 1, p. 246.

1. Ø   4. Ø   7. Ø
2. as   5. from   8. Ø
3. Ø   6. to

◇ PRACTICE 2, p. 246.

1. the same as   6. similar to
2. the same   7. different from
3. similar   8. similar to
4. similar   9. different
5. different   10. different from

◇ PRACTICE 3, p. 247.

1. English is different from Japanese.
   English and Japanese are different.
2. Trains and buses are similar.
   Trains are similar to buses.
3. Your grammar book is the same as my grammar book.
   Your grammar book and my grammar book are the same.
4. Women and men are different.
   Women are different from men.

◇ PRACTICE 4, p. 247.

1. like   4. like   7. like
2. alike   5. alike   8. alike
3. alike   6. like   9. alike

◇ PRACTICE 5, p. 248.

Answers may vary:
1. Nurses are like doctors. They help people.
2. White chocolate and dark chocolate are alike. They are sweet.
3. Magazines are like newspapers. They have articles.
4. Scissors and knives are alike. They are sharp.
5. Malaysia and Thailand are alike. They are hot.
6. Ice-cream cones are like milkshakes. They are delicious.
7. Chemistry and physics are alike. They are sciences.

◇ PRACTICE 6, p. 248.

1. younger than   10. more expensive than
2. wider than   11. easier than
3. cheaper than   12. funnier than
4. darker than   13. better than
5. smarter than   14. farther/further than
6. older than   15. fatter than
7. happier than   16. hotter than
8. more important than   17. thinner than
9. more difficult than   18. worse than

◇ PRACTICE 7, p. 249.

1. warmer than   9. better than
2. funnier than   10. worse than
3. more interesting than   11. prettier than
4. smarter than   12. more confusing than
5. more famous than   13. farther/further . . . than
6. wider than   14. better than
7. larger than   15. easier than
8. darker than   16. more beautiful than

◇ PRACTICE 8, p. 250.

Sample answers:
1. 101A is more interesting than 101B.
2. 101B is more boring than 101A.
3. 101B is harder than 101A.
4. 101A is easier than 101B.
5. 101A is more popular than 101B.
6. 101B is more difficult than 101A.
7. 101A is more enjoyable than 101B.

◇ PRACTICE 9, p. 251.

Sample answers:
1. Life in the country is quieter than life in the city.
2. Life in the city is more expensive than life in the country.
3. Life in the suburbs is more relaxing than life in the city.
4. Life in the city is busier than life in the country.
5. Life in the suburbs is more convenient than life in the country.
6. Life in the country is more beautiful than life in the suburbs.
7. Life in the country is cheaper than life in the city.

8. Life in the country is nicer than life in the city.
9. Life in the suburbs is safer than life in the city.
10. Life in the country is better than life in the city.

◇ **PRACTICE 10, p. 252.**

	Comparative	*Superlative*
1.	more expensive than	the most expensive
2.	lazier than	the laziest
3.	cleaner than	the cleanest
4.	older than	the oldest
5.	younger than	the youngest
6.	newer than	the newest
7.	more beautiful than	the most beautiful
8.	more exciting than	the most exciting
9.	nicer than	the nicest
10.	quieter than	the quietest
11.	worse than	the worst
12.	fatter than	the fattest
13.	thinner than	the thinnest
14.	hotter than	the hottest
15.	better than	the best
16.	cheaper than	the cheapest
17.	farther than	the farthest

◇ **PRACTICE 11, p. 252.**

1. . . . hardest . . .
2. . . . most beautiful . . .
3. . . . most interesting . . .
4. . . . most boring
5. . . . easiest . . .
6. . . . most talented . . .
7. . . . most relaxing . . .
8. . . . best . . .

◇ **PRACTICE 12, p. 253.**

Sample answers:
1. A 5-star restaurant is the most expensive.
2. A fast-food restaurant is the most convenient.
3. A 5-star restaurant is the most relaxing.
4. A fast-food restaurant is the busiest.
5. A 5-star restaurant is the nicest.
6. An Internet café is the most interesting.
7. A fast-food restaurant is the most popular.
8. An Internet café is the quietest.
9. A fast-food restaurant is the cheapest.
10. An Internet café is the most useful.

◇ **PRACTICE 13, p. 254.**

Sample answers:
1. Fluffy is the laziest.
   Fluffy is lazier than Rex.
2. Rex is the most active.
   Rex is more active than Polly.
3. Fluffy is the youngest.
   Fluffy is younger than Rex.
4. Rex is the heaviest.
   Rex is heavier than Polly.
5. Polly is the most colorful.
   Polly is more colorful than Fluffy.
6. Rex is the biggest.
   Rex is bigger than Polly.
7. Polly is the oldest.
   Polly is older than Fluffy.
8. Polly is the smallest.
   Polly is smaller than Rex.
9. Polly is the lightest.
   Polly is lighter than Rex.

◇ **PRACTICE 14, p. 255.**

1. the hottest months
2. the fastest cars
3. the happiest couples
4. the funniest children
5. the best teachers
6. the tallest women
7. the oldest men
8. the most interesting people/persons
9. the scariest animals

◇ **PRACTICE 15, p. 256.**

Sample answers:
1. Running is one of the easiest sports to learn.
2. Skydiving is one of the most dangerous sports.
3. Golf is one of the most expensive sports.
4. Race-walking is one of the safest sports.
5. Skiing is one of the most difficult sports.
6. Baseball is one of the most interesting sports.
7. Swimming is one of best sports for your heart.

◇ **PRACTICE 16, p. 256.**

Answers may vary.
1. Lichtenstein is one of the smallest countries in the world.
2. . . . is one of the biggest cities.
3. . . . is one of the hardest languages to learn.
4. . . . is one of the most interesting places to visit.
5. . . . is one of the prettiest places to visit.
6. . . . is one of the most expensive cities to visit.
7. . . . is one of the most important people/persons in the world.

◇ **PRACTICE 17, p. 257.**

1. the biggest
2. longer than
3. the hottest places
4. the coldest places
5. larger than
6. the largest
7. the longest
8. The smallest
9. the scariest
10. the most dangerous animals

◇ **PRACTICE 18, p. 258.**

1. slow
2. cold
3. hard
4. complicated/difficult/hard
5. short
6. cheap/inexpensive
7. comfortable
8. cool
9. heavy
10. new

◇ **PRACTICE 19, p. 258.**

1. aren't
2. can
3. do
4. don't
5. doesn't
6. wasn't
7. will
8. does
9. didn't
10. don't
11. is
12. can't
13. won't
14. are
15. was
16. did
17. aren't

◇ PRACTICE 20, p. 259.
Sample answers:
1. cats don't.
2. cows don't.
3. people can't.
4. flowers do.
5. the weather is the mountains isn't.
6. happiness (education/good health/etc.) is.
7. expensive things aren't.
8. is/isn't.

◇ PRACTICE 21, p. 259.

Adjective	*Adverb*	*Comparative*	*Superlative*
1. quick	quickly	more quickly	the most quickly
2. clear	clearly	more clearly	the most clearly
3. slow	slowly	more slowly	the most slowly
4. beautiful	beautifully	more beautifully	the most beautifully
5. neat	neatly	more neatly	the most neatly
6. careful	carefully	more carefully	the most carefully
7. fluent	fluently	more fluently	the most fluently
8. good	well	better	the best
9. hard	hard	harder	the hardest
10. early	early	earlier	the earliest
11. late	late	later	the latest
12. fast	fast	faster	the fastest

◇ PRACTICE 22, p. 260.
1. more beautifully than
2. more carefully than
3. the most quickly
4. the hardest
5. later than
6. the earliest
7. better than
8. more quickly than
9. more slowly than
10. the most fluently
11. faster than
12. the best

◇ PRACTICE 23, p. 260.
1. heavier than
2. more dangerous than
3. more dangerously than
4. the most dangerously
5. more clearly than
6. clearer than
7. the most clearly
8. harder than
9. the hardest
10. better than
11. the best
12. better than
13. longer than
14. the longest
15. neater than
16. more neatly than

◇ PRACTICE 24, p. 261.
1. A
2. B
3. C
4. A
5. D
6. B
7. C
8. C
9. B
10. A
11. A
12. D

NOTES

NOTES

NOTES

NOTES